Kok Loang Ooi

Demystifying Behavioral Finance

Foundational Theories to Contemporary Applications and Future Directions

Springer

Kok Loang Ooi
Department of Finance
Faculty of Business and Economics
University of Malaya
Kuala Lumpur, Malaysia

ISBN 978-981-96-2689-2 ISBN 978-981-96-2690-8 (eBook)
https://doi.org/10.1007/978-981-96-2690-8

This Springer imprint is published by the registered company Springer Nature Singapore Pte Ltd.
The registered company address is: 152 Beach Road, #21-01/04 Gateway East, Singapore 189721, Singapore

My family's constant support and encouragement have served as the basis for my path.

To my mentors and coworkers who have inspired me with their knowledge and advice. And to all the interested minds delving into the interesting field of behavioral finance, may this book inspire fresh thoughts and insights.

Preface

Welcome to Demystifying Behavioral Finance: Foundational Theories to Contemporary Applications and Future Directions, an in-depth look at the psychology that drives financial markets. This book will lead you through the vital, often hidden factors that affect investor behavior, impact market patterns, and threaten the fundamental foundations of conventional finance. In these pages, we'll look at the exciting topic of behavioral finance, delving into complicated ideas, and relating them to real-world events and future financial trends.

Finance has long been seen as a realm of precise statistics, facts, and logical decision-making. However, as you'll soon find, the truth is much more intricate. Markets are influenced by human behavior—biases, emotions, and occasionally illogical impulses. Behavioral finance is the area that investigates these psychological factors, providing insights that go beyond mathematics to explain the fundamental nature of financial decision-making. This book allows you to go further into these concepts, giving you the information you need to understand markets from a new perspective.

Our trip is structured into three segments, each shedding light on a different facet of behavioral finance. Let's take a short look at what's in store.

Part I: Foundations of Behavioral Finance

We begin with the origins of behavioral finance, tracking the field's progress from its most groundbreaking concepts. Foundations of Behavioral Finance exposes you to the groundbreaking ideas and thinkers that dared to challenge orthodox finance. Prospect Theory and mental accounting are two concepts that illustrate the biases and irrationalities that underpin financial decision-making. These chapters take you back to the beginnings of the discipline when behavioral economists discovered patterns that traditional models could not explain. You'll learn how these fundamental ideas undermined the "rational investor" assumption and paved the way for a new understanding of finance. This part isn't simply about the past; it's about comprehending the fundamental concepts that still drive the subject now.

Part II: Behavioral Finance in Today's Markets

With our basis set, we go forward to the present, where behavioral finance has emerged as an essential lens for evaluating contemporary markets. In Behavioral Finance in Today's Markets, we look at how biases and psychological inclinations affect investment choices today. You'll learn about cognitive traps, including overconfidence, herd behavior, and loss aversion, as well as how they affect trading methods, investing decisions, and market movements. This section brings the ideas to life with case studies of contemporary financial events, ranging from the Dot-com Bubble and the 2008 Financial Crisis to the recent volatility in the cryptocurrency market. These chapters demonstrate how behavioral finance ideas apply in real-world circumstances, explaining the frequently chaotic and unexpected behavior of today's markets. By the conclusion of this lesson, you'll understand behavioral finance not just as a theoretical framework but also as a valuable tool for identifying market movements and managing risk.

Part III: The Future of Behavioral Finance

Finally, we look forward to The Future of Behavioral Finance, a segment that investigates how technological innovation is transforming the subject. As artificial intelligence, big data, and machine learning gain traction in financial systems, behavioral finance provides an essential lens through which to interpret these developments. This section investigates the convergence of psychology and technology, specifically how AI technologies and data analytics are used to forecast investor behavior while admitting that human biases remain at the core of market dynamics. In these chapters, we also look at the global component of behavioral finance, namely how cultural influences influence financial behavior in various areas. This section finishes with a consideration of the policy implications of behavioral finance, imagining a future in which insights from this subject may aid in the creation of more stable and resilient markets. As finance becomes more global and linked, behavioral finance will play an essential role in creating legislation, safeguarding investors, and leading financial innovation.

Each section of this book builds on the previous one, resulting in a complete picture of behavioral finance, from its fundamental ideas to present applications and future possibilities. By the conclusion, you'll not only comprehend the fundamentals of behavioral finance but also recognize its transformational influence on finance as a whole. Whether you're an investor, a student, or just interested in the psychology of decision-making, this book will shift your perspective on markets and the forces that drive them.

Kuala Lumpur, Malaysia

Kok Loang Ooi

Acknowledgment

Writing this book has been an amazing experience, and it would not have been possible without the help and contributions of several people and organizations. First and foremost, I want to convey my heartfelt thanks to my family. Their patience, support, and love have been a source of strength for me during this journey. I am genuinely grateful to my mentors and colleagues for shaping my knowledge of behavioral finance and inspiring me with their ideas. I want to express my profound gratitude to the students and researchers who questioned my beliefs, extended my perspectives, and inspired me to explore further into the subtleties of investor behavior and market dynamics. I am thankful to Universiti Malaya, for giving the resources and assistance that enabled the creation of this work. Finally, I want to thank my readers for their interest in this intriguing topic. I hope this book helps you comprehend and negotiate the complex interaction between psychology and money.

Competing Interests The author has no competing interests to declare that are relevant to the content of this manuscript.

About this Book

Demystifying Behavioral money: Foundational Theories to Contemporary Applications and Future Directions examines the complex relationship between psychology and money, revealing the psychological factors influencing market behavior. This book explores the progression of behavioral finance, including its fundamental ideas, revolutionary effects on modern markets, and future prospects.

The first section examines the foundations of behavioral finance, revealing innovative ideas such as Prospect Theory and mental accounting that challenged the conventional "rational investor" paradigm. It underscores significant abnormalities such as loss aversion and herd behavior, demonstrating how emotions and biases permeate financial decision-making, resulting in market inefficiencies and volatility.

The second section of the book shifts to contemporary markets, illustrating practical applications of behavioral finance via case studies such as the Dot-com Bubble, the 2008 Financial Crisis, and the emergence of cryptocurrencies. These chapters examine the impact of cognitive biases such as overconfidence and anxiety on trading behavior, providing pragmatic insights for maneuvering through the sometimes tumultuous and unexpected financial environment.

The last portion examines the future of behavioral finance, investigating the intersection between technology and psychology. It analyzes the impact of artificial intelligence, machine learning, and big data on stock selection, risk management, and market forecasting, while also considering the issues new technologies provide, including ethical dilemmas and systemic concerns. This part also examines the global views of behavioral finance, highlighting the impact of cultural and regional differences on financial behavior.

This book serves as a thorough resource for financial professionals, students, and everyone interested in the psychology of decision-making. It offers a sophisticated comprehension of the influence of human behavior on financial markets, arming readers with the skills to address biases, reduce risks, and capitalize on opportunities in a constantly changing financial landscape. Demystifying Behavioral Finance bridges the gap between theory and practice, enabling readers to reconsider their financial engagement and cultivate a more educated and resilient investment strategy.

Contents

About the Author

Kok Loang Ooi is a leading expert in finance, celebrated for his deep insights into behavioral finance and his broad contributions to academia and industry. Currently a faculty member in the Department of Finance at Universiti Malaya, ranked 60th in the 2025 QS World University Rankings, Dr. Ooi previously served as Deputy Dean at City University Malaysia. He holds a Master's and Ph.D. in Finance from Universiti Sains Malaysia (USM) and a Master of Laws from the International Islamic University Malaysia (IIUM), reflecting a rich academic foundation across finance and legal studies.

Dr. Ooi's extensive professional background includes advising Malaysia's top 100 listed companies and serving as a board advisor, where he provided strategic insights on finance and corporate governance. His early career as an auditor and business consultant at KPMG, one of the Big Four accounting firms, equipped him with a robust understanding of corporate finance and market strategy. He is a Certified Internal Auditor (CIA) and a Professional Member of the Institute of Internal Auditors, further strengthening his expertise in regulatory and compliance aspects of finance.

Over the past five years, Dr. Ooi has published more than 40 influential papers in high-impact journals, including *Finance Research Letters*, *Journal of Economic Studies*, *The Singapore Economic Review*, *International Journal of Islamic and Middle Eastern Finance and Management*, and *China Finance Review International*. His research delves into behavioral biases like herding, overconfidence, and overreaction, challenging traditional finance theories and reframing investor behavior through a psychological lens.

A dedicated mentor, Dr. Ooi has successfully guided over 25 PhD students to graduation, fostering the growth of future finance leaders. He regularly shares his expertise with central banks, financial institutions, and on major platforms such as China Talk Show. Dr. Ooi's unique combination of academic depth, industry acumen, and regulatory knowledge continues to redefine and elevate the field of behavioral finance, offering critical perspectives on the psychological forces that shape global markets.

List of Figures

List of Tables

Part I
The Past

Imagine entering a world where financial theories were governed by the idea of the 'rational investor', someone who made judgements based entirely on statistics, was emotionally detached, and was resistant to errors. However, when markets swung from elation to fear, and bubbles swelled and then fell, it became evident that real-life investors did not follow this logical script. Part I: The Past delves at the roots of behavioral finance, a subject that evolved to explain the human aspect of finance, challenging previously held strict beliefs.

In this section, we'll return to the groundbreaking theories and concepts that debunked the notion of simply rational markets. Why do we cling to losing investments for longer than we should? What drives investors to follow the majority even when logic suggests they shouldn't? And why do fear and greed seem to take root when the stakes are the highest? This section highlights the foundation of a discipline that integrated human psychology into finance by presenting early notions like loss aversion and behavioural biases, demonstrating that markets are driven by emotion and instinct as much as logical calculation.

The principles in the past provided the framework for a new approach to finance—one that saw investors as actual people, replete with idiosyncrasies, prejudices, and urges that may derail even the most meticulously designed financial models. As we explore these fundamental principles, we realise why knowing the fundamentals of behavioural finance is critical: they remind us that underneath every stock chart and financial model is the unexpected power of human nature. As you read, think about how these themes still apply today. Could understanding the biases that formed behavioural finance from the beginning be the answer to managing today's complicated markets?

Chapter 1
Early Concepts and Theories

Imagine the excitement of a rising market when optimism is infectious, riches seem endless, and everyone feels they can ride the wave to the top. Consider the chaos of a market collapse when the same traders who felt invincible yesterday are now anxious to flee with everything they can save. Why does the market's attitude change so dramatically? And why do even experienced investors make illogical decisions?

Human nature, rather than statistics, algorithms, or models, holds the key to the solution.

Welcome to *Demystifying Behavioural Finance: Foundational Theories to Contemporary Applications and Future Directions*, an exploration of the psychological dynamics that shape financial markets. This book peels back the layers of conventional finance to expose a world in which emotions, prejudices, and herd instincts drive choices as much as statistics and logic. In these pages, you will understand why we are lured to danger, why we follow the herd, and why we often make the same errors, no matter how much we learn.

For decades, finance was based on the idea that investors are rational and accurately assess risks and rewards. However, the actual market is anything but reasonable. It is a human behaviour theatre where fear, greed, and hope play out their daily dramas, shaping fortunes and driving market swings. Behavioural finance reveals this underlying tale, highlighting the peculiarities and urges that may lead to both success and calamity.

This book will take you on a journey through the most dramatic periods in financial history, from the dot-com bubble to the 2008 Financial Crisis, cryptocurrency booms, and beyond. Each of these occurrences was more than just a money incident; they were psychological phenomena. As you read, you will discover how a combination of overconfidence, herd behaviour, and pure terror may cause wild market swings, resulting in turmoil and opportunity for those who can see past the noise.

However, *Demystifying Behavioural Finance* is more than just a history lesson. It serves as a guidebook for the future. As we approach a new age in which artificial

K. L. Ooi, *Demystifying Behavioral Finance*,
https://doi.org/10.1007/978-981-96-2690-8_1

intelligence and big data promise to anticipate market patterns with greater accuracy, behavioural finance presents a critical counterpoint. Technology may alter the way we trade, but it will not change our identities. Understanding the biases, anxieties, and instincts that drive investor behaviour is critical for navigating the complicated world of contemporary finance—and this book provides precisely that.

If you are a trader, this book will teach you how to identify—and avoid—your psychological pitfalls. If you are a finance student, you will learn about a discipline that is changing the way we think about markets. If you are just curious about human behaviour, you will learn about the psychological dynamics that create one of our life's most significant venues.

This is *Demystifying Behavioural Finance*—an exploration of the human brain at the core of finance, from basic ideas to today's most important financial concerns and the future. Prepare to delve beyond the statistics to uncover the actual factors driving the financial world.

Traditional finance theories have long served as the foundation for understanding financial markets, providing structured models that assume rational and efficient investment choices. These theories are founded on the assumption that investors behave rationally, attempting to maximise profits while minimising risk via systematic appraisals of information. For decades, ideas such as the efficient market hypothesis (EMH), modern portfolio theory (MPT), and the capital asset pricing model (CAPM) have influenced not just academic thinking but also the practical ways that investors and institutions take to asset management (Baek & Lee, 2021). The basic assumption in these theories is that markets are orderly and predictable, adapting to new information swiftly and without prejudice.

However, as financial markets expanded, so examined these fundamental beliefs. While traditional finance models have provided valuable frameworks for understanding investment behaviour, their assumptions about perfect rationality and efficient markets frequently fail to explain real-world anomalies such as bubbles, crashes, and the impact of psychological biases on investor behaviour (Fama, 1970). Nonetheless, these ideas are still important in finance, acting as critical instruments for risk assessment, portfolio design, and asset pricing. By going into the ideas of EMH, MPT, and CAPM, we may discover the fundamental logic that still underpins most of today's investing strategy, even as behavioural finance challenges these assumptions. Table 1.1 provides a concise comparison of foundational financial theories, highlighting their core principles, implications, and limitations.

Table 1.1 Foundational financial theories

Concept/theory	Key points
Efficient market hypothesis (EMH)	• Stock prices reflect all relevant information instantly • Divided into three forms: weak, semi-strong, and strong Weak form: Historical data is priced in, making technical analysis ineffective Semi-strong form: Prices incorporate all public information, challenging fundamental analysis Strong form: Prices reflect all public and private information, negating insider advantages
	• Highlights 'information symmetry' where markets respond instantly to news • Criticised for ignoring anomalies like speculative bubbles and behavioural biases • Real-world evidence often deviates due to irrational behaviour and delayed reactions
Modern portfolio theory (MPT)	• Introduced by Harry Markowitz in 1952 • Focuses on diversification to minimise risk and maximise returns • Introduces the efficient frontier, representing optimal risk-return portfolios Emphasises the importance of asset allocation over stock picking • Inspired passive investment strategies like index funds and ETFs
	• Limitations include reliance on historical data, assumptions of rational behaviour, and correlation breakdowns during crises • Criticised for oversimplifying risk management but remains foundational in investment strategies
Capital asset pricing model (CAPM)	• Not included in this summary per request, as it focuses solely on APT and EMH
Arbitrage pricing theory (APT)	• Developed by Stephen Ross in 1976 as a multifactor model for asset pricing • Asset returns are influenced by multiple factors, such as inflation, GDP growth, and interest rates • Relies on arbitrage forces to correct mispricing • Provides flexibility to adapt factors based on specific contexts, such as emerging markets or niche industries
	• Implementation challenges include identifying relevant factors, estimating betas, and accounting for real-world frictions (e.g. transaction costs, liquidity) • Highlights the complexity of risk-return dynamics and provides a customisable framework for decision-making

1.1 Efficient Market Hypothesis

The efficient market hypothesis is at the heart of classical finance, a theory that has shaped financial thought for decades. Eugene Fama's EMH theory claims that in an efficient market, stock prices completely and instantly reflect all relevant information. This theory is founded on the assumption that in competitive markets, investors utilise available data to make optimum choices, guaranteeing that any new information about a stock—whether a fresh earnings report, economic projection, or geopolitical event—is swiftly absorbed into its price. According to EMH, it is impossible to continually outperform average market returns since stock prices always represent their underlying worth.

EMH is often represented using the concept of 'information symmetry'. Assume a corporation launches a revolutionary product at 9:00 a.m. Within seconds, traders all across the globe react to this news, buying up shares until the stock price increases to represent the product's expected earnings. By 9:01, the stock's new price had already included this knowledge, leaving little possibility for investors to profit from it further. Proponents of EMH say that the continual flow of information results in price efficiency, in which no one investor has an edge over others, rendering market timing or stock selection inefficient. Although commonly recognised, EMH has been criticised for ignoring market anomalies, such as speculative bubbles, in which prices diverge dramatically from underlying values, implying that efficiency is an ideal rather than an absolute reality.

Imagine you are in Times Square on New Year's Eve, surrounded by thousands of people all watching the same events on a large screen. In a moment, news flashes across the screens: a pharmaceutical firm has created a remarkable new therapy for a life-threatening condition. Within seconds, this information is broadcast all across the world, not just in Times Square (Heath & Tversky, 1991). Traders in London, Tokyo, and New York are responding in real time, as are the markets. The company's stock price skyrockets almost immediately, reflecting the widespread conviction that this discovery would result in enormous profits.

This is the core of the EMH, which states that in an efficient market, stock prices instantly reflect all relevant information. According to EMH, it is practically difficult to 'beat the market' on a continuous basis since any advantage acquired by analysing information is already included in the stock price at the time it becomes public. Eugene Fama, who created this theory, describes the stock market as a highly efficient mechanism that absorbs new data at breakneck speed. Every piece of breaking news, whether it is an earnings report, a product launch, or a geopolitical event, has innumerable analysts, traders, and algorithms ready to modify their tactics, resulting in a fast recalibration of pricing.

Take the dot-com bubble as an example. During the late 1990s, technology stocks skyrocketed as investors saw the Internet's transformational potential. However, according to EMH, these price increases were justified by all available data—until they were not. When the bubble burst in the early 2000s, stock prices fell as the market swiftly responded to fresh information indicating that many firms were overpriced and lacked viable revenue strategies. EMH would claim that, even during this tumultuous time, prices represented all available information, albeit the theory is often criticised for failing to account for irrational exuberance and unexpected collapses. EMH is based on the premise of rationality (DellaVigna, 2009). Still, real-world anomalies like the dot-com disaster show that markets, although frequently efficient, are not immune to human emotions and group behaviour.

The weak form of EMH posits that all historical market data, including prices, trading volumes, and patterns, are already reflected in current asset prices. This suggests that technical analysis, which relies on historical price trends and chart patterns to predict future movements, is largely ineffective in gaining a consistent edge over the market. Proponents argue that any advantage derived from analysing past data is quickly neutralised as investors act on it, ensuring no predictable patterns remain exploitable.

Imagine a trader named David, who is a staunch believer in technical analysis. He spends hours dissecting charts, identifying head-and-shoulders patterns, and back-testing moving averages. One day, David notices that a tech stock has recently formed a 'double bottom', a pattern traditionally associated with an impending price rally. He confidently places a large buy order, expecting significant profits. However, instead of rallying, the stock dips further due to an unexpected announcement of regulatory scrutiny. What went wrong? Under weak form efficiency, the stock's historical data—the foundation of David's analysis—offered no predictive power because the market had already absorbed and acted on that information. The sudden dip was driven by new, unforeseen developments, rendering his analysis moot.

Critics of the weak form argue that anomalies, such as momentum effects (where past winners continue to perform well for some time), challenge its validity. Studies have shown that certain strategies exploiting historical patterns can outperform the market temporarily. However, such strategies often lose their effectiveness as they gain popularity and competition increases. While weak form efficiency provides a solid baseline, it does not entirely dismiss the possibility of short-lived inefficiencies in the market (Odean, 1998).

The semi-strong form of EMH builds on the weak form by asserting that asset prices incorporate not only historical data but also all publicly available information. This includes financial statements, news releases, economic forecasts, and even social media chatter. The semi-strong form challenges the efficacy of fundamental analysis, as it assumes that the market swiftly and accurately incorporates all relevant public information into prices. Investors who rely on analysing public data are unlikely to consistently outperform the market because any new information is already 'priced in'.

Consider Emma, a meticulous investor who prides herself on digging into annual reports and listening to earnings calls. She discovers that a consumer goods company has reported record-breaking quarterly sales, and she quickly decides to buy shares, anticipating a sharp price increase. However, by the time she executes her trade, the stock's price has already spiked. What Emma did not realise is that the market had anticipated this earnings announcement weeks earlier, with analysts and investors factoring in the company's strong performance based on prior sales trends and industry projections (Huberman, 2001). The semi-strong form suggests that Emma's fundamental analysis was futile because the public information she acted on was already reflected in the stock's price.

Nevertheless, the semi-strong form is not without its detractors. Behavioural biases, delayed reactions, and market overreactions suggest that public information is not always immediately and accurately incorporated into prices. For example, during times of market panic, even strong earnings reports may fail to prevent a stock from declining as investors prioritise fear over facts. Similarly, bubbles—like the dot-com bubble of the late 1990s—often see prices soar far beyond what public fundamentals would justify. These deviations highlight the tension between the theoretical efficiency of markets and the behavioural realities of human decision-making.

The strong form of EMH is the most ambitious and controversial, claiming that all information—public and private—is fully reflected in asset prices. In this idealised world, even insider information offers no advantage because the market has already accounted for it (Shiller, 2000). This implies that no investor, regardless of their resources, expertise, or privileged access, can consistently outperform the market.

Imagine a hedge fund manager named Alex, who receives a tip from an insider at a biotech company about an upcoming FDA approval for a breakthrough drug. Confident that this information will yield significant profits, Alex purchases shares ahead of the announcement. However, when the FDA approval is made public, the stock barely moves. To Alex's dismay, the market had already priced in the high probability of approval based on earlier statements from the company and analysts' projections. The strong form of EMH suggests that Alex's insider knowledge provided no edge because the collective market had already incorporated all available and implied information.

While strong form efficiency offers an elegant theoretical framework, real-world evidence casts doubt on its feasibility. Insider trading scandals, such as those involving high-profile executives and hedge funds, demonstrate that non-public information can indeed confer significant advantages. Additionally, opaque markets and illiquid securities often defy the principles of strong form efficiency, creating opportunities for informed players to exploit inefficiencies. For these reasons, many scholars and practitioners view the strong form as more of an intellectual exercise than a practical reality.

1.2 Modern Portfolio Theory

Developed by Harry Markowitz in 1952, MPT introduced a systematic approach to constructing an investment portfolio that balances risk and return through diversification. CAPM, introduced by William Sharpe in the 1960s, built on MPT's concepts by establishing a formal relationship between an asset's expected return and its systematic risk. Together, these theories revolutionised investment strategy and asset pricing, but their practical implications and limitations continue to fuel academic and professional debate (Lo, 2004). Harry Markowitz established modern portfolio theory (MPT), which changed the way investors think about risk and diversity. MPT suggests that investors may create an 'efficient portfolio' that maximises returns for a given degree of risk by carefully choosing an asset mix. MPT believes that diversification—combining assets with varied correlations—can be used to minimise portfolio risk since asset values do not always move in tandem. For example, in instances when stock values fall, bond prices may stay steady or even climb, providing a buffer against losses. MPT revolves around the idea of the 'efficient frontier', which is a curve that represents optimum portfolios with the most significant potential return-to-risk ratio.

Consider Emma, an investor. Emma likes tech stocks because of their growth potential, but she is aware that they may be volatile. If she only invests in high-growth technology, her portfolio might fluctuate substantially when the market evolves. She may, however, lessen the volatility of the portfolio by diversifying into stable, income-generating bonds, real estate investment trusts (REITs), and perhaps some defensive equities such as utilities. By mixing assets with varied degrees of risk and correlation, she is bringing her portfolio closer to the efficient frontier.

The practical implications of MPT are significant. It shifted the focus of investment management from individual asset performance to portfolio construction, underscoring that asset allocation is more critical than stock picking. Institutional investors, such as pension funds and mutual funds, rely on MPT principles to balance their portfolios between high-risk and low-risk assets. For example, a portfolio may combine equities for growth potential with government bonds for stability, ensuring the portfolio aligns with the efficient frontier and reflects the investor's risk tolerance (Wermers, 1999).

Additionally, MPT laid the groundwork for passive investment strategies. The theory's emphasis on market efficiency and diversification inspired the creation of index funds and ETFs, enabling investors to achieve broad exposure to asset classes with low fees. MPT also helped popularise the use of metrics such as standard deviation and correlation in assessing portfolio risk, making these tools standard in financial planning and investment analysis.

However, MPT has its limitations. It assumes that investors are rational and risk-averse, that markets are efficient, and that asset returns follow a normal distribution—all assumptions that do not always hold in practice. For instance, during market crises, asset correlations often increase, diminishing the diversification benefits MPT promises. Moreover, reliance on historical data for estimating returns and volatilities can lead to flawed projections when market conditions change. Behavioural biases, such as overconfidence and loss aversion, also challenge the rational decision-making assumptions of MPT. These limitations have prompted the evolution of alternative models, such as behavioural portfolio theory and adaptive asset allocation, which attempt to incorporate real-world complexities into portfolio management.

MPT became a core concept in finance because it promoted diversification—investing in several assets rather than focussing on a single, high-reward opportunity. The idea recognises that, although risk cannot be removed entirely, it may be controlled by careful asset selection. Critics of MPT say that it is too reliant on past data and fails to account for extraordinary occurrences when correlations across asset classes converge. For example, during the 2008 financial crisis, even typically low-risk investments such as bonds saw losses. Nonetheless, MPT's primary concept remains immensely relevant, showing investors how a diverse portfolio may help smooth the way through complicated financial terrain (Wermers, 1999).

1.3 Capital Asset Pricing Model

William Sharpe established the capital asset pricing model (CAPM), which is a systematic technique to evaluate the connection between risk and anticipated return for specific assets. According to CAPM, an asset's expected return is defined by its sensitivity to market risk, or beta (β), which reflects how much the asset's price fluctuates compared to the market. The model implies that investors demand compensation not just for the time value of money but also for accepting more risk, which is represented by the market risk premium. The CAPM formula—anticipated return = risk-free rate + (beta × market risk premium)—enables investors to determine the expected return for a given amount of systematic risk.

Let us return to Alex and Jamie to show CAPM. Assume they are contemplating two stocks: Stock A, a utility business with a low beta of 0.6, and Stock B, a tech start-up with a high beta of 1.8. The CAPM recommends that Stock B should have a higher anticipated return to compensate for its higher volatility. Using CAPM's method, both friends may determine if each stock's predicted return is worth the risk. For example, if the risk-free rate is 3% and the market risk premium is 5%, the CAPM predicts that Stock A (with a beta of 0.6) should offer an anticipated return of 6% (3% + 0.6 × 5%), but Stock B (with a beta of 1.8) should yield an expected return of 12% (3% + 1.8 × 5%).

CAPM is very effective for valuing equities and determining if the rewards justify the risk. For example, a high-beta stock that fluctuates more violently with the market is predicted to provide more significant returns than a low-beta one with more consistent price changes. Using CAPM, an investor may determine if a high-risk stock is likely to deliver returns that compensate for its volatility. While CAPM has become a finance industry standard, with analysts and fund managers using it extensively, it has limits. CAPM presupposes that all investors have access to the same information and have diverse portfolios, which is different in practice. Furthermore, CAPM's dependence on beta as the primary measure of risk has been criticised since it does not account for variables other than market movements that may impact returns. Nonetheless, CAPM remains an essential tool in asset pricing and is critical to understanding the risk-return trade-off in conventional banking (Baker & Ricciardi, 2014).

Other classic finance theories depict a logical, ordered universe in which markets function smoothly and investors make sound judgements. Consider the dividend discount model (DDM), which evaluates a company by computing the present value of future payments. In principle, it is a dependable formula—until a catastrophe like 2008 occurs. Suddenly, once-reliable payouts are reduced, and DDM's calm assumptions disintegrate as investors panic, witnessing their projected cash flows evaporate overnight. Similarly, random walk theory posits that stock values follow a random, independent pattern in response to new information. However, at times of crisis, such as the COVID-19 collapse, prices do not move independently; instead, they fall in lockstep as dread grabs investors throughout the globe. What remains is a market swept by psychological contagion, which contradicts the theory's assumption of isolated, random movements.

1.4 Arbitrage Pricing Theory

Arbitrage pricing theory (APT) is a paradigm shift in understanding the dynamics that determine asset values, providing a multidimensional lens through which to observe the complex dance of risks and rewards in financial markets. APT, developed by Stephen Ross in 1976, boldly moved away from the constraints of single-factor explanations and into the complexity of the actual world. It emphasises that market movements are seldom driven by a single overarching element but rather by a symphony of forces ranging from macroeconomic shocks to industry trends and firm-specific dynamics. The beauty of APT rests in its exquisite simplicity combined with deep explanatory power: the notion that arbitrage pressures, like invisible hands, guarantee that assets are valued in accordance with their genuine risk exposures.

At its foundation, APT is a mathematical representation of the market's balancing process. It asserts that an asset's anticipated return is defined by its sensitivities, or betas, to a variety of economic and market-wide variables. Each element reflects a distinct source of systematic risk, such as unanticipated fluctuations in inflation, GDP growth, interest rates, or commodity prices. The idea succinctly proposes that if an asset's price deviates from the return justified by its exposure to these variables, arbitrageurs—investors who profit from price differences—will rush in. Their transactions will push the market back into equilibrium, removing any chance for risk-free returns.

Consider Laura, an investor who specialises in spotting mispriced stocks in developing nations. She notes that a manufacturing company in Brazil is trading below its theoretical value due to its vulnerability to global commodity prices, interest rates, and local currency fluctuations. According to APT, this disparity is a gold ticket. Laura buys the shares, hoping that when other investors see the mispricing, the price would climb to represent its real worth. Within weeks, her gamble pays off, as the stock rises just as APT predicted. APT's fascination and strength stem from the market's self-correcting process, which is powered by arbitrage.

The consequences of APT extend well beyond the realm of theoretical finance. By recognising numerous sources of risk, APT gives a more complex framework for making financial decisions. Consider a portfolio manager who manages a worldwide equities fund. Unlike single-factor models, which may only account for broad market patterns, APT allows this manager to analyse the portfolio's exposure to particular risks such as oil price swings, geopolitical tensions, and alterations in global trade policy. With this level of insight, the manager may make more educated decisions, such as hedging against oil price volatility by adding energy equities or minimising exposure to politically problematic countries. In this sense, APT becomes more than simply a pricing tool; it also serves as a strategic compass.

One of APT's most appealing qualities is its versatility. Unlike rigid models, which prescribe a predefined set of variables, APT enables practitioners to customise their analysis to the unique scenario under consideration. For example, in the unpredictable world of technology companies, variables such as innovation cycles and venture capital flows may have a greater impact than standard economic indicators. This adaptability has made APT important in narrow markets and specialised industries, where standard frameworks often fall short (Kumar, 2009).

Despite its attraction, installing APT is not an easy task. One of the most difficult difficulties is identifying the key elements that determine asset pricing. The idea does not specify what these characteristics should be, allowing researchers and practitioners to decide which hazards are most important. The answer often varies depending on the market, time period, and assets in issue. For example, during periods of economic instability, factors such as inflation or interest rate shocks may gain precedence, but in stable times, industry-specific variables may take centre stage. While ambiguity provides freedom, it also requires significant judgment and skill, making APT both an art and a science.

Another problem is evaluating each asset's sensitivity—or beta—to the stated parameters. This need reliable data, advanced statistical tools, and cautious interpretation. Errors in estimating may lead to mispricing, diminishing the arbitrage possibilities that APT aims to explain. Furthermore, in real-world markets, frictions such as transaction costs, liquidity limits, and regulatory hurdles may stymie the arbitrage process, enabling mispricing to remain longer than the theory suggests (DellaVigna, 2009).

However, these problems do not reduce APT's brilliance; rather, they highlight its intricacy. By embracing financial market complexity, APT allows for a more in-depth knowledge of the dynamics that drive asset values. It reminds us that investing is more than just responding to market movements; it is also about discovering the deep web of linkages between risks and profits. Imagine a world in which artificial intelligence and massive data propel APT to new heights. Advanced algorithms capable of evaluating millions of data points in real time make detecting key elements and predicting betas more exact than before. Investors using these technologies might identify arbitrage opportunities with surgical precision, bringing the theoretical beauty of APT closer to reality. This future is not far off; in many respects, it is already here, as quantitative and hedge funds incorporate multifactor models inspired by APT into their trading methods.

1.5 The Rational Investor Myth

Consider a world in which every investor functions like a well-oiled machine, calculating each move with immaculate logic and foresight. The rational investor laid the groundwork for classical finance theory. According to this viewpoint, each market player was an unstoppable force of logic, motivated purely by the quest for profit and the capacity to calculate risks precisely. This investor was immune to emotion, never affected by fear or greed, and was always looking for the highest return with the least amount of risk. Economists expected markets to run smoothly and reliably because, with rational investors in charge, prices would always represent the actual worth of things.

This confidence in rationality was more than just a notion; it served as the foundation for models such as the efficient market hypothesis, which believed that all available information was immediately and precisely integrated into stock prices, leaving no space for surprises or mistakes. However, reality quickly proved different. As markets surged and plummeted in ways that defied logic, economists realised something profound: investors were human, and their behaviour was unpredictable.

Consider the 1929 collapse. Investors poured their resources into a soaring stock market, believing that prices would only rise. However, as fear struck, the same mob rushed to sell, resulting in a catastrophic collapse. The reasonable investor would not have pursued a bubble, nor would they have rushed to the exits at the first hint of danger. These occurrences highlighted a crucial problem in previous models: they failed to account for human behaviour. And they so started the path into behavioural finance. This discipline would alter finance by recognising that every stock price is the result of a human being with emotions, biases, and impulses that cannot be measured (Laibson, 1997).

Table 1.2 provides an overview of key behavioural finance theories, emphasising their central concepts and implications for investor behaviour. These theories highlight the psychological biases and mental shortcuts that often lead to irrational decision-making in financial markets. For example, prospect theory explains the emotional weight of losses compared to gains, while mental accounting reveals how individuals compartmentalise money, leading to inconsistent financial behaviour. Anchoring bias, overconfidence, and herd behaviour further illustrate how cognitive limitations and social influences can distort judgement.

Table 1.2 Behavioural finance theories and their implications

Theory	Key concept	Implications
Prospect theory	Individuals feel the pain of losses more intensely than the pleasure of equivalent gains. Decisions are influenced by perceived reference points rather than objective outcomes	Explains why investors often avoid risks when faced with potential losses, even if holding could yield better long-term rewards. Demonstrates the emotional weight of losses in decision-making
Mental accounting	People divide their money into mental 'accounts' based on origin or purpose, treating identical sums differently depending on their context	Leads to irrational financial behaviour, such as excessive spending of windfalls while neglecting long-term goals. Demonstrates the compartmentalisation of financial decision-making
Anchoring bias	Initial information (an 'anchor') heavily influences subsequent decisions, even if it is arbitrary or irrelevant	Causes investors to cling to outdated reference points, leading to missed opportunities or poor investment decisions based on irrelevant anchors

(continued)

Table 1.2 (continued)

Theory	Key concept	Implications
Overconfidence bias	Overestimation of one's abilities or knowledge leads to excessive risk-taking and disregard for market realities	Results in frequent trading, increased risk exposure, and resistance to acknowledging market realities, often culminating in significant financial losses
Herd behaviour	Investors follow the actions of the majority, often without understanding the rationale, driven by the fear of missing out or panic	Inflates market bubbles and exacerbates crashes as collective actions create momentum detached from fundamentals. Demonstrates the power of group psychology over individual analysis
Representativeness heuristic	People judge new investments based on their resemblance to past successful ones, often ignoring critical differences	Leads to unrealistic expectations and overvaluation of assets, often resulting in losses when the assumed patterns fail to materialise
Bounded rationality	Decision-making is limited by time, cognitive resources, and incomplete information, causing investors to settle for 'good enough' rather than optimal choices	Encourages reliance on shortcuts and heuristics, which can lead to suboptimal decisions, especially in complex or dynamic market conditions
Availability heuristic	Decisions are disproportionately influenced by recent, vivid, or memorable events rather than objective probabilities	Skews risk perception and decision-making, leading to chasing trends or excessive caution, depending on the availability of positive or negative recent experiences

1.6 Prospect Theory: Why Losses Hurt More Than Gains

In the 1970s, two psychologists, Daniel Kahneman and Amos Tversky, set out to investigate a perplexing question: Why do individuals experience losses more profoundly than gains? Through a series of pioneering tests, they found that individuals need to balance risks and rewards logically. They respond significantly more strongly to losses than to similar benefits. This finding inspired them to create prospect theory, which became one of the most prominent concepts in behavioural finance (Heath & Tversky, 1991).

To understand this notion, envision Sarah as a young investor. Sarah's portfolio is performing well, and she is excited to see her profits expand. But one day, a market slump wipes off a chunk of her gains. Although Sarah is aware that markets fluctuate, the sight of her balance falling below its high fills her with fear. She is losing more than just money; she is losing something she previously thought was hers, and the anguish is enormous. Despite her long-term ambitions, Sarah has concentrated on preventing additional downturns, selling her assets at a loss rather than keeping them stable.

Kahneman and Tversky discovered that the pain of loss, or loss aversion, is a universal tendency. In financial terms, it implies that the dread of losing $100 outweighs the joy of receiving the same amount. This observation prompted them to create the notion of reference reliance, in which people judge outcomes depending on a perceived reference point. For Sarah, the reference point represents the most outstanding value in her portfolio. Falling below it seems like a failure, and she is more prone to make rash choices to prevent future 'losses', even if they are just temporary (Laibson, 1997).

Prospect theory provides a novel viewpoint: individuals do not make financial choices by objectively assessing all alternatives. They are motivated by their fear of loss, which often leads them to take solutions that guard against perceived risks rather than maximise prospective advantages. This simple but significant finding altered economists' understanding of investor psychology, demonstrating that every transaction is driven by a highly personal fight between fear and reward.

1.7 Mental Accounting: Why We Treat Money Differently

Assume you have gotten a tax return and consider this money 'extra'. Instead of putting money in your savings account, you choose to spend it on a luxurious weekend excursion. After all, this is not your average salary; it is a bonus—free money. Welcome to the realm of mental accounting, a notion that describes how individuals mentally split their money into distinct 'accounts' depending on its origin, purpose, or other characteristics rather than considering all currencies equally (Gervais & Odean, 2001).

To learn how mental accounting works in finance, meet John, an investor with a retirement savings fund. When it comes to his monthly salary, John is highly disciplined, constantly depositing a percentage of it into his retirement account. But one day, he gets a significant profit from a stock he gambled on. This unexpected income felt like a jackpot for him. Instead of reinvesting or adding it to his retirement savings, he uses it as 'fun money' and buys a new sports automobile he has always wanted.

Although rewarding in the short term, this behaviour exposes a cognitive quirk: John sees his investment gain as fundamentally distinct from his regular income, enabling him to spend it more freely. Mental accounting demonstrates that individuals compartmentalise money into 'buckets', with one kind being spent more freely than another. This attitude leads to illogical decisions, such as using bonuses or tax refunds to indulge while keeping 'serious' money in a savings account.

For investors like John, mental accounting might have long-term consequences. By cognitively categorising windfalls as different, people risk jeopardising their financial objectives and taking rash actions that do not correspond with their long-term ambitions. Behavioural finance demonstrates how these internal mental 'accounts' may skew our perception of money, leading us to make choices that fulfil immediate demands but fall short of ideal financial planning.

1.8 Anchoring Bias: The Power of First Impressions in Finance

Anchoring bias is an unseen force that may influence financial choices without our knowledge. The idea is simple yet effective: once we receive an initial piece of information—a figure, a price, or an estimate—it acts as an 'anchor' in our thoughts. Future decisions gravitate towards this initial anchor, even if it is arbitrary or irrelevant.

Assume Lisa is an investor who is interested in a potential technology stock. When she initially comes across it, the price is $50 per share, and she takes a mental note of that as her starting point. A few months later, the stock is up to $70. Lisa understands that $70 may still be a reasonable price, but she hesitates because it seems 'too expensive' in comparison to her first reference of $50. In her opinion, $50 is the genuine 'value' of the company, and any price beyond that seems inflated, even if market circumstances have changed. Conversely, if the stock fell to $40, it is a bargain, even if the loss was caused by unfavourable adjustments in the company's fundamentals.

This anchoring bias significantly impacts investor behaviour because consumers become fixed on a specific price point, influencing their propensity to purchase or sell. Once established, the first number serves as a psychological standard for all subsequent judgements. For Lisa, this $50 anchor affects her view of worth, preventing her from correctly determining whether $70 reflects progress or just increased expectation.

In the financial realm, anchoring bias may cause significant distortions. Investors may stay with early values or expectations that are no longer applicable. This might result in overpaying for equities that have grown above their fair worth or, conversely, selling cheap stocks at a loss because they are 'anchored' to a higher price. Anchoring demonstrates that in finance, initial impressions are crucial. Once a number is established, it is difficult to change, often driving actions that contradict both logic and market reality.

1.9 Overconfidence Bias

Consider a trader called Daniel, who has had a successful year in the market. He began modestly, buying a few equities in rising industries like technology and energy. With each good deal, his confidence increased. He came to feel he had an intuitive understanding of the market—a unique, even magical, capacity to predict winners. By the end of the year, Daniel was riding high, believing that he had a particular skill that went beyond plain chance. He informed others about his method, looked down on 'average' investors, and even began offering unsolicited advice. He felt he had overcome the market's ups and downs. Overconfidence had taken hold, fuelling an obsessive feeling of control over something that was essentially unmanageable.

Overconfidence bias is more than simply believing in oneself; it is the subtle but firm belief that you know more than everyone else. With each successful deal, the trader begins to feel remarkable rather than just adept. They look at market patterns and believe they can find connections that others cannot. They make more significant deals, take on greater risk, and disregard indications that might have warned them in the past. Daniel's portfolio swelled, and he started to leverage his holdings, borrowing to acquire additional companies, convinced that his unique insight would keep him safe. But overconfidence is a dangerous thing—it creates a bubble around the investor, insulating them from the reality that markets are unpredictable and complicated, much beyond any one person's comprehension.

The market eventually took a turn, as it typically does. The stocks that had previously surged started to fall. Daniel hung on, confident they would recover, unable to recognise the indicators that the tide had altered. After all, he believed he was the exception. Overconfidence causes investors to think they are in control despite mounting evidence to the contrary. When Daniel eventually began selling, it was too late—the losses had wiped out all of his earnings, plus some. He was left with the sour taste of arrogance, seeing that his so-called talent was mostly chance riding a favourable market cycle (Königstorfer & Thalmann, 2020).

Overconfidence reminds us how harmful an unbridled ego can be in the financial world. It blinds investors to the exact dangers that characterise the market, causing them to trade too often, disregard warning signs, and eventually suffer the consequences of their overreach. In finance, humility is a virtue, but arrogance is a weakness that may lead to disaster. Daniel's narrative is all too common: a cycle of self-assured triumph followed by a stunning breakdown, a sobering reminder that the market rewards respect over recklessness.

1.10 Herd Behaviour

Imagine passing through a busy market square and seeing a small group of people sprinting towards a particular vendor. They seem energetic and active, and more people join them, attracted by the rush. Without understanding why, you feel compelled to participate, not wanting to lose out on whatever is attracting this gathering. In investing, the impulse to follow others—herd behaviour—is a tremendous, almost primitive force. It is what motivates individuals to purchase when everyone else is buying and to sell when everyone else is selling, even if they do not entirely see why. Herd behaviour may seem to be a shortcut to certainty, but it often leads investors into bubbles and disasters, fuelled by mass momentum rather than critical research.

Herd behaviour feeds on communal excitement, the perception that everyone else sees something you do not. When a stock or asset gains popularity, it causes a domino effect in which each new buyer drives up the price, making investing look even more appealing. Investors who might usually hesitate are drawn in, thinking they will miss an excellent chance. It is the 'fear of missing out' turned into a frenzy. The more individuals purchase, the greater the herd's pull and prices increase, regardless of any underlying fundamentals. The tendency reinforces itself, and investors defend their decisions by citing growing prices, mistaking popularity for value.

When the bubble breaks, the herd reacts just as quickly, and the rush for the exits is immediate and savage. Those who entered late find themselves with expensive assets, racing to sell before values plummet further. This massive sell-off is motivated by the same mentality that drove the purchasing frenzy: following the herd. However, the crowd's excitement has turned to fear, and the market responds appropriately, with prices plunging as everyone attempts to cash out at the same time. It is a phenomenon that has occurred throughout history, from the 1600s Tulip Mania to the 2008 housing market meltdown, in which herd behaviour caused millions of people to suffer financial ruin (Raimundo Júnior et al., 2022).

Herd behaviour demonstrates the effectiveness of collective psychology in finance. The crowd's efforts give a beguiling appearance of safety, but they actually multiply dangers, inflating bubbles and hastening disasters. Following the crowd may seem safe, even sensible, yet herd behaviour is mainly motivated by psychology rather than reason. It serves as a reminder that in the world of money, following the crowd is not always the best option. In reality, it is often a formula for catastrophe, with the crowd pushing investors over the brink in search of something they do not want to miss but do not fully comprehend.

1.11 Representativeness Heuristic

Imagine seeing a new business take off, with stock prices slowly rising over a few quarters. The firm is inventive, making headlines, and you begin to imagine it resembles Google or Amazon in their early days. The representativeness heuristic is a mental shortcut for seeing a pattern in a current investment and connecting it to a previous success story, regardless of the underlying differences. It is the instinct that says, 'This stock looks like a winner because it resembles past winners', without checking to see whether that likeness holds up under investigation.

Representativeness encourages investors to depend on preconceptions, making judgements based on perceived patterns rather than actual evidence. In finance, this refers to investing in high-growth stocks or hot industries solely because they seem to be the 'next big thing'. However, this mental shortcut might be deceptive. For every Google or Amazon, numerous more firms had a similar early trajectory but eventually failed to generate long-term value. The representativeness heuristic blinds investors to the intricacies that distinguish each firm and market environment, causing them to make unduly optimistic predictions.

The issue of the representativeness heuristic is that it generates hype cycles. Investors go after high-flying equities, believing they have discovered the next superstar, while in truth, they are buying into exaggerated expectations. This bias causes investors to miss fundamentals like cash flow, debt, and competitive posture, instead focusing on superficial similarities. During the cryptocurrency boom, for example, several new currencies and tokens seemed to replicate Bitcoin's stratospheric increase, prompting investors to jump in, believing these assets would follow suit. However, when prices plummeted, it became evident that only some cryptocurrencies were destined to emulate Bitcoin's success (Baek & Lee, 2021).

This heuristic is a trap that entices investors with the promise of replicating history's greatest successes. However, finance does not function that way—several factors impact markets, and no two organisations or assets are precisely comparable. The representativeness heuristic tempts investors to detect patterns where none exists, to assume that history will repeat itself without taking into account the variances that might result in a very different conclusion. It serves as a compelling reminder that in markets, making assumptions based on familiarity may be expensive.

1.12 Bounded Rationality

Bounded rationality is a humble idea. It acknowledges that, no matter how smart or knowledgeable we are, our capacity to digest information is limited. Consider a seasoned portfolio manager poring through mounds of information—earnings reports, economic indicators, and market projections. In an ideal world, they would carefully analyse each piece of information. But in fact, they do not have that luxury. Time is limited, cognitive resources are restricted, and instead of making ideal judgements, people often settle for 'good enough' ones. This is the essence of limited rationality.

In finance, constrained rationality explains why even knowledgeable investors may make judgements based on insufficient facts or mental shortcuts. Instead of analysing every detail, they concentrate on essential indications or metrics, using proxies to guide their decisions. This strategy is efficient, but it has a cost. By restricting their attention, investors can make sure they get all critical information and signals that might influence their choice. Bounded rationality is like driving in a fog—you see part of the road, but you are constantly aware that there may be something hidden just ahead, which you will not realise until it is too late.

During moments of significant volatility, limited rationality is much more apparent. Investors stick to what they know, focusing on known companies or safe sectors in an attempt to handle uncertainty with a restricted perspective of the terrain. Instead of thoroughly examining each choice, they settle for options that seem 'good enough' under the circumstances. However, this tendency might make investors susceptible to shocks. Relying on shortcuts may work in stable markets, but in times of crisis, when information is constantly changing, it can lead to expensive mistakes.

Bounded rationality emphasises that perfect knowledge and flawless choices are illusions. In finance, investors face limits, making judgements based on incomplete information and limited time. The irony is that although constrained rationality allows us to make faster decisions, it also leaves room for mistakes, particularly when markets become uncertain. It is a sobering thought, a reminder that in the pursuit of profit, every investor is navigating with half information, hoping that their restricted viewpoint will keep them out of trouble.

1.13 Availability Heuristic

The availability heuristic is a mental shortcut in which recent or remembered events have an undue impact on decision-making. Imagine hearing about a stock that has soared overnight; it is thrilling, vivid, and memorable. Now, when you contemplate investing, that memory acts as a filter, driving you to pursue similar chances, even if they are riskier. In finance, the availability heuristic causes investors to concentrate on the most recent trends or high-profile news, skewing their perception of likelihood based on what is fresh in their minds rather than what is genuinely probable (Barber & Odean, 2000).

This bias may lead to illogical actions, such as investing money in a flourishing industry without fully appreciating the hazards. If an investor saw a buddy benefit from a tech stock, they may assume tech is a sure option since the success story is so compelling. However, this shortcut blinds consumers to the larger market reality, the cyclical nature of sectors, and the many variables that influence stock performance. The availability heuristic produces a restricted viewpoint in which current events trump a balanced view, causing investors to rush into trends they hardly grasp.

During market downturns, the availability heuristic might have the reverse effect, causing excessive caution. Investors who a previous catastrophe has damaged may shun stocks entirely, believing that the same slump will occur again. This bias causes people to overestimate the frequency of recurrence incidents, focusing on worst-case scenarios rather than recovery probabilities. It is why many investors lost out on the post-2008 bull market, clinging to memories of the catastrophe and disregarding long-term growth indicators. The availability heuristic keeps individuals stuck in the past, distorting their view of danger and opportunity.

In finance, the availability heuristic reminds us that our judgements are seldom objective. We depend on what is vivid, current, and emotionally charged, even when additional evidence recommends a different option. This bias promotes reactive behaviour, in which investors pursue the newest trends or worry about recent losses while failing to understand the big picture. It is a mental shortcut that may lead to costly blunders, a stark reminder that in markets, what is most remembered is not often what is most important.

As we conclude this introduction to the psychological basis of investing, one thing becomes clear: our brains are not designed for the rationality and accuracy that standard finance theories predict. The biases we have investigated—overconfidence, herd mentality, representativeness, limited rationality, and the availability heuristic—show that we are not the rational agents that those theories predict. Instead, reflexes, mental shortcuts, and occasionally illusions of control influence our judgements in unanticipated ways. Each of these biases exposes another layer of financial psychology, indicating that enormous psychological factors are at work behind every purchase or sale, frequently acting against us (Glaser & Weber, 2007).

This is more than simply a curiosity; it represents a fundamental change in how we see markets. Traditional finance theories imply that prices are logical, investors are rational, and markets accurately represent all available information. However, a closer examination reveals a different reality: one in which investors are often carried up by emotion, making illogical decisions, and moving in herds. This flawed, biased behaviour causes market inefficiencies—when prices soar too high, plummet too low, or follow patterns that contradict conventional explanations. Our human faults influence the marketplaces in which we work.

In Chap. 2, we will go from theory to real-world examples, investigating how these biases cause market inefficiencies and behavioural abnormalities. We will look at how investor psychology creates asset bubbles, fuels speculative frenzy, and causes market collapses. These are not single events; they are part of a larger pattern in which our collective irrationality influences market cycles in ways that orthodox finance cannot wholly explain. Get ready because we are going to witness how powerful—and occasionally chaotic—our prejudices can be when they collide on the market stage.

References

Baek, S., & Lee, K. Y. (2021). The risk transmission of COVID-19 in the US stock market. *Applied Economics, 53*(17), 1976–1990.

Baker, H. K., & Ricciardi, V. (2014). How biases affect investor behaviour. *The European Financial Review, 7*(1), 7–10.

Barber, B. M., & Odean, T. (2000). Trading is hazardous to your wealth: The common stock investment performance of individual investors. *The Journal of Finance, 55*(2), 773–806.

DellaVigna, S. (2009). Psychology and economics: Evidence from the field. *Journal of Economic Literature, 47*(2), 315–372.

Fama, E. F. (1970). Efficient capital markets: A review of theory and empirical work. *Journal of Finance, 25*(2), 383–417.

Gervais, S., & Odean, T. (2001). Learning to be overconfident. *The Review of Financial Studies, 14*(1), 1–27.

Glaser, M., & Weber, M. (2007). Overconfidence and trading volume. *The Geneva Risk and Insurance Review, 32*(1), 1–36.

Heath, C., & Tversky, A. (1991). Preference and belief: Ambiguity and competence in choice under uncertainty. *Journal of Risk and Uncertainty, 4*(1), 5–28.

Huberman, G. (2001). Familiarity breeds investment. *The Review of Financial Studies, 14*(3), 659–680.

Königstorfer, F., & Thalmann, S. (2020). Applications of Artificial Intelligence in commercial banks–A research agenda for behavioral finance. *Journal of Behavioral and Experimental Finance, 27*, 100352.

Kumar, A. (2009). Who gambles in the stock market? *The Journal of Finance, 64*(4), 1889–1933.

Laibson, D. (1997). Golden eggs and hyperbolic discounting. *The Quarterly Journal of Economics, 112*(2), 443–478.

Lo, A. W. (2004). The adaptive markets hypothesis: Market efficiency from an evolutionary perspective. *The Journal of Portfolio Management, 30*(5), 15–29.

Odean, T. (1998). Are investors reluctant to realize their losses? *The Journal of Finance, 53*(5), 1775–1798.

Raimundo Júnior, G. D. S., Palazzi, R. B., Tavares, R. D. S., & Klotzle, M. C. (2022). Market stress and herding: A new approach to the cryptocurrency market. *Journal of Behavioral Finance, 23*(1), 43–57.

Shiller, R. J. (2000). *Irrational exuberance*. Princeton University Press.

Wermers, R. (1999). Mutual fund herding and the impact on stock prices. *The Journal of Finance, 54*(2), 581–622.

Chapter 2
Behavioural Anomalies and Market Inefficiencies

In a perfect world, markets reflect pure logic, with prices rising and falling in response to facts, projections, and reasonable analysis. However, in fact, markets could be more efficient, driven by waves of emotion, instinct, and collective judgement that defy conventional models. Behavioural anomalies create deep-rooted inefficiencies in the system, distorting pricing and causing periods of irrational exuberance or panic that standard finance theories cannot explain. These inefficiencies are not just small ripples; they are tremendous, destabilising forces that may transform steady expansion into soaring bubbles and careful corrections into catastrophic disasters (Coval & Shumway, 2005).

Price anomalies, or instances when asset prices deviate from their fundamental values, are one of the most apparent symptoms of market inefficiency. Consider a software business that explodes onto the scene with a new app, attracting hordes of eager investors. Its future revenues are unknown, its user base is limited, and its business model needs to be better tested. However, as enthusiasm spreads, the stock price soars. Investors, enthralled by the prospect of the next great thing, drive the price ever higher, far above what its fundamentals would imply. This price anomaly does not represent the company's true worth; rather, it indicates market optimism and, eventually, weakness (Ben-David et al., 2013). When prices grow disconnected from actual worth, they produce a market prone to rapid corrections, where exaggerated confidence may shift into widespread selling at the first sign of negative news.

These price anomalies do not simply cause bubbles in individual equities; they also contribute to market volatility. Consider the market to be a tranquil lake, with prices moving gently and rationally. However, when investors are motivated by fear or greed, the ripples become waves, shifting prices drastically in both directions. During bull markets, enthusiasm may drive prices skyrocketing as investors join in, confident that the uptrend will never stop. Then, when uncertainty seeps in—perhaps due to an economic report or an unexpected earnings miss—the market may plummet, with investors rushing to sell in order to prevent more losses. This

K. L. Ooi, *Demystifying Behavioral Finance*,
https://doi.org/10.1007/978-981-96-2690-8_2

increased volatility is not indicative of an efficient market; instead, it demonstrates collective irrationality, in which the fear of loss and the desire for gain cause price fluctuations much beyond what the statistics would suggest. Volatility creates a self-perpetuating loop in which extreme variations feed on one other, pushing prices farther away from their inherent values (Kumar, 2009).

Another result of these behavioral inefficiencies is resource misallocation. When investor sentiment inflates some sectors, such as tech during the dot-com bubble or real estate before the 2008 crisis, money floods into them, often at the cost of more stable ones. Investors, driven by the desire to maximise profits, pour money into speculative initiatives with excessive valuations and unproven business concepts. At the same time, sectors with consistent growth and sound fundamentals should be considered. This misallocation of resources has far-reaching consequences. Companies that would not have lasted in a reasonable market get generous finance, while successful enterprises need help to obtain money. When the bubble eventually collapses, these overhyped industries see a dramatic capital flight, resulting in lay-offs, bankruptcies, and economic contractions. It is not only investors who suffer; whole sectors may be rattled, and the larger economy often suffers the consequences of this capital loss.

These inefficiencies do not just stop with bubbles and corrections; they often grow into full-fledged market collapses, inflicting lasting scars on investor confidence and the economy as a whole. Bubbles are constructed on a frail foundation: the idea that prices will continue to rise, the crowd will continue to buy in, and value will always match with investor excitement. But when reality catches up—whether via disappointing profits, a shift in economic policy, or a global event—the bubble bursts, causing a chain reaction. Investors, suddenly seized by fear, rush to sell, sending prices further down (Statman, 2017). The crisis does more than merely reset asset values; it shatters the sense of stability, resulting in widespread losses that may take years to recoup. Crashes expose the market's weakness, demonstrating that inefficiencies are not innocuous quirks—they are fractures that, when enlarged, cause economic turmoil.

Human emotion is at the heart of almost all market inefficiencies. In principle, investors are meant to behave rationally, analysing facts and assessing risks. However, when the stakes are significant, emotions such as fear, greed, and excitement often outweigh rationality. Emotional decision-making is a tremendous force that pushes prices away from their actual worth, causing both bubbles and collapses. When investors witness increasing prices, greed takes control, and the fear of losing out motivates them to purchase at any cost. They persuade themselves that this is the new normal, that prices will increase eternally, even when logic indicates otherwise.

Conversely, as prices begin to decline, panic sets in. Investors who had previously faith in the stability of their holdings are now panicking, hurrying to sell and minimising losses. It is not that they have learnt new facts; instead, they are responding to the emotional sensation of losing their riches. This emotional decision-making may cause prices to skyrocket—or plummet—far below what fundamentals would suggest.

Consider an investor called Alex, who has seen his money continuously expand throughout a bull market. His confidence has grown over the years, and he is confident that his plan is sound. But one morning, he wakes up to find that the market has dropped by 5%. Red numbers flash over his screen, and all the information he previously believed disappears into the background. He can only concentrate on one thing: his shrinking portfolio. Panic sets in, overpowering the rational counsel he knows so well. He sells despite having pledged himself to hold. By the end of the day, he has locked in his losses, and the market is beginning to rebound. Alex's choice was based solely on emotion—his fear of losing money exceeded his belief in his method. When you multiply Alex's experience by thousands of investors, you have a market that is driven by fear rather than fundamentals, with prices reflecting worry instead of value.

Although information is the market's currency, it is only available to some. Information asymmetry arises when some investors have access to information that others still need. In a world where everyone has the same knowledge, prices would move evenly, reflecting a shared idea of worth. However, certain players often have insights that give them a significant advantage, resulting in inefficiencies as prices fluctuate in reaction to the privileged few. Consider insider trading, which involves executives and other insiders acting on sensitive information. While the larger market stays in the dark, insiders may buy or sell based on their knowledge, causing prices to change before the information is made public (Hirshleifer, 2015). This discrepancy causes inefficiencies since prices are determined by insufficient knowledge. By the time regular investors catch up, the early traders have already gained, and the entire market sees price movements that are not based on publicly available information.

Consider Sarah, an investor with a buddy who works at a pharmaceutical business that is set to unveil a breakthrough medicine. Sarah learns that this medicine is likely to gain FDA clearance, which will send the stock skyrocketing. She buys shares surreptitiously, awaiting the public announcement. A few days later, when the news breaks, the stock price skyrockets, and Sarah profits handsomely. What is her advantage? She knew before anybody else. Because of information asymmetry, Sarah was able to act on information that others lacked. The market's response to her activities prompted prices to skyrocket, but it did not accurately represent the stock's worth. It was an inefficiency caused by the benefit of insider information.

When emotions combine with insufficient knowledge, herd behaviour often results. Humans are social beings, and in markets, this means following the herd, particularly during times of uncertainty. Herd behaviour is the propensity of people to copy the acts of the majority, thinking that the group knows something they do not. The collective momentum propels asset values to unsustainable highs or shattering lows, resulting in inefficiencies that defy reasonable explanations. Herd behaviour is most noticeable during speculative bubbles, when prices rise due to communal excitement rather than inherent worth. Investors see others purchasing and are concerned about missing out. Soon, everyone is jumping on the bandwagon, driving up costs. However, when sentiment swings, the herd flees, panicking and selling. Prices plummet due to a change in group psychology rather than fresh facts.

Herd behaviour reinforces emotional decision-making, transforming individual impulses into market-wide occurrences.

Remember the late-1990s dot-com bubble? Jake, a novice investor, observes that everyone around him seems to be earning billions by investing in technology companies. Companies with little profits are seeing their stock values double or triple overnight. Jake is still determining the basics, but he feels the draw of the audience. His friends are investing, the media is buzzing, and he cannot escape the notion that he will regret not participating. He buys in, confident he has discovered his way to riches. But as the bubble bursts, the herd shifts from buying to selling, and Jake sees his profits disappear. Herd behaviour, driven by fear of losing out rather than critical analysis, has kept him holding overvalued equities in a sinking market. The illogical urge of the mob generated a brief sense of affluence, disguising the inefficiency that was about to be exposed.

Overconfidence is a powerful and often concealed source of market inefficiency. When investors feel they have particular insight or a unique capacity to anticipate the market, they become overconfident, disregarding dangers and taking on too many holdings. Overconfident investors trade too often, believing they can predict every high and low. They ignore caution indicators, believing that their previous triumphs are evidence of their ability rather than chance. Overconfidence distorts prices because it causes investors to purchase and sell based on incorrect assumptions. Overconfident traders control large areas of the market, and prices reflect their inflated opinions rather than their true worth. As a consequence, overconfidence often drives prices to unsustainable heights, resulting in bubbles that inevitably collapse, leaving a path of losses when reality reclaims control.

Meet Tom, a day trader with a successful year. His confidence rises with each successful deal, and he starts to feel he has an advantage over the rest of the market. He begins placing larger wagers, thinking that he can 'see' patterns that others cannot. When his pals warn him, he rejects them, claiming, 'I know what I'm doing'. However, as the market takes an unforeseen turn, his holdings begin to unravel. Overconfidence drove Tom to take needless risks, increasing his portfolio and ego beyond what reality could support. His anecdote serves as a warning that market overconfidence may result in prices that represent hubris rather than actual value, and when such illusions shatter, inefficiencies follow (Gervais & Odean, 2001).

The human brain is hardwired for shortcuts, particularly in complicated situations like banking. These mental shortcuts, known as heuristics, assist us in making speedy judgements but may result in cognitive biases that affect judgement. For example, the representativeness heuristic leads investors to believe that a rising stock will continue to rise only based on previous performance. Similarly, the availability heuristic overestimates the likelihood of recent or noteworthy occurrences, causing investors to overreact to a recent fall or rise.

These cognitive biases create inefficiencies by causing investors to respond to patterns that do not always anticipate future events. When enough investors follow these prejudices, the market becomes distorted, with prices reflecting psychological proclivities rather than value. Cognitive biases demonstrate that inefficiencies are firmly ingrained in our thinking since investors base their judgements not on analysis but on mental shortcuts that reduce complexity.

Consider Mary, an investor who has had consistent profits in the stock market for many years. She begins to assume that the upward trend will continue forever, and she buys more aggressively, confident that her stocks will continue to perform. But as the market begins to fall, she clings to the belief that it is just a temporary setback, dismissing warning indications of an economic crisis. Her reliance on prior trends caused her to invest more than necessary, locking her in a market decline she might have averted. Mary's narrative demonstrates how cognitive biases such as representativeness may cause investors to inflate prices, resulting in inefficiencies that go undetected until reality destroys the illusion.

In a society that values quarterly outcomes, both businesses and investors concentrate on short-term success. This short-term concentration causes inefficiencies because organisations make choices to satisfy shareholders in the near term, which frequently comes at the price of long-term progress. Investors, in turn, respond strongly to quarterly earnings reports, buying and selling based on modest variations rather than the company's long-term prospects. This short-term concentration causes violent price movements, with stocks rising and falling with each earnings announcement. When markets are based on quarterly data rather than fundamentals, prices reflect transient outcomes rather than genuine value, resulting in market inefficiencies.

Consider a tech CEO preparing for an earnings call. Under pressure to meet quarterly objectives, she reduces research investment to increase immediate earnings. Investors praise the action, driving up the stock price despite the fact that the company's long-term potential has been harmed (Lo, 2004). Each quarter, the cycle repeats, with prices reflecting short-term gains rather than long-term growth. This emphasis on quarterly results reflects a market driven by transient success, a fragile system with inefficiencies built into every earnings report.

2.1 Dot-Com Bubble in 2000

The late 1990s were electrifying—a moment when the promise of the Internet infused every conference room and trading floor with a feeling of certainty. The concept was simple and seductive: the Internet would transform every element of life, and those who invested early would benefit from a historic wealth explosion (Hirshleifer, 2015). Tech businesses sprang suddenly, with values rising nearly as quickly as the founders' goals. Between 1995 and 2000, the Nasdaq Composite Index increased by 566%, from roughly 750 points to over 5000. The world watched as technology stocks skyrocketed, and anybody with a computer or a dream believed they, too, could be the next billionaire.

But under the surface of this exhilaration was a worrying inefficiency. Investors poured money into firms that had no earnings, no income, and, in many cases, no actual business strategy other than a concept and a catchy dot-com name. Take Pets.

com, which debuted in 1998 with the goal of revolutionising pet supplies buying. With millions of dollars in advertising and a now-iconic sock puppet mascot, Pets. com generated $82.5 million in its first public offering in 2000. However, the firm was haemorrhaging cash, losing money on every order, and there needed to be an obvious road to profitability. However, investors required more (Barberis & Thaler, 2003). Pets.com's stock skyrocketed to $11 per share, only to drop to $0.19 9 months later when reality took hold. By November 2000, Pets.com and numerous other Internet businesses had failed, bringing with them the hopes—and fortunes—of millions.

Figure 2.1 highlights the NASDAQ Composite Index during the dot-com bubble (1995–2000). At the core of the bubble was a collective suspension of rational financial judgement. Many of the companies that garnered investor attention had little more than a catchy name or a vague business plan. Firms such as Pets.com, which promised to revolutionise pet supply retailing, became icons of the era. Pets.com raised $82.5 million in its 2000 IPO, bolstered by aggressive marketing campaigns and a widely recognised sock puppet mascot. Despite its popularity, the company haemorrhaged money, losing on every transaction due to high operational costs and thin profit margins. By November 2000, the company had collapsed, and its stock price fell from an initial $11 per share to just $0.19. Pets.com was not alone; many internet start0ups, lacking sustainable business models, succumbed to similar fates as the market corrected.

The decline of the Nasdaq Composite Index was as dramatic as its ascent. By October 2002, the index had fallen by approximately 78% from its peak, erasing more than $5 trillion in market capitalisation. This massive downturn highlighted the perils of speculative bubbles driven by herd behaviour and irrational exuberance. Investors who had once believed in boundless growth saw their portfolios

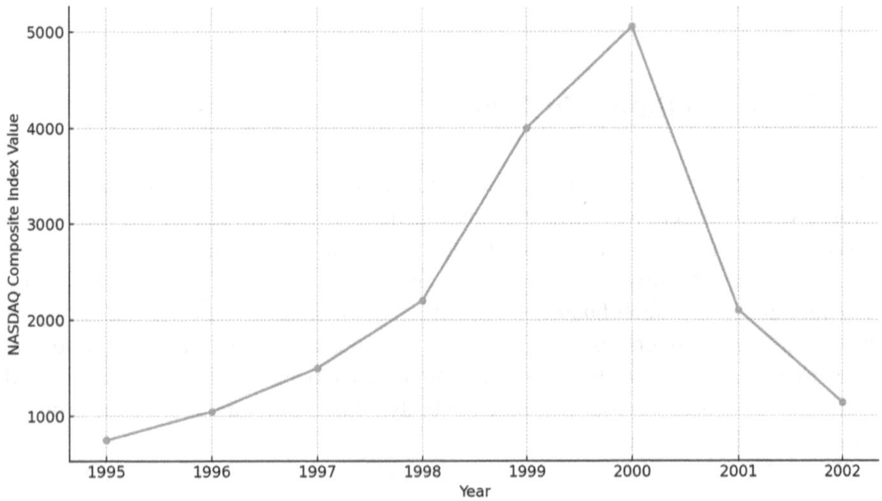

Fig. 2.1 NASDAQ Composite Index during the dot-com bubble (1995–2000)

decimated. The financial fallout extended beyond individual investors, as institutional funds, retirement accounts, and venture capital investments also suffered severe losses. The bursting of the bubble exposed the fragility of a market detached from fundamental valuation principles.

The dot-com bubble serves as a classic case study in market inefficiency and behavioral finance. During the bubble, herd behaviour played a critical role as investors followed the crowd, often without fully understanding the risks. The fear of missing out (FOMO) further amplified speculative behaviour, driving prices to unsustainable levels. Many investors rationalised their decisions by pointing to rising prices, mistaking momentum for value. This speculative frenzy created a feedback loop: rising prices attracted more investors, which in turn drove prices even higher, perpetuating the illusion of limitless growth.

When the bubble burst, the psychological dynamics reversed. Panic replaced optimism, and investors scrambled to sell their holdings, leading to a sharp and widespread market decline. This period of capitulation demonstrated the dangers of overconfidence, as many investors had believed their strategies were foolproof. It also underscored the role of cognitive biases, such as anchoring and availability heuristics, in distorting investment decisions. Investors anchored their expectations to the rapid gains of the late 1990s, and the vivid memory of the crash reinforced overly cautious behaviour in the years that followed.

The fall was quick and severe. By 2002, the Nasdaq had dropped about 78% from its high, wiping off more than $5 trillion in market value. Investors who had joined the frenzy believing in infinite development were astonished to see that prices had gone outrageously out of proportion to reality. The dot-com bubble was a typical illustration of market inefficiency at scale—a period when herd behaviour, excessive optimism, and the abandonment of fundamentals resulted in a market buoyed up by delusion. When the bubble burst, it was not only corporations that suffered; whole portfolios, retirement funds, and ambitions vanished almost quickly, exposing the actual cost of a market inflated by hype rather than value.

2.2 US Housing Bubble and 2008 Financial Crisis

If the dot-com bubble was founded on the idea of digital change, the 2008 housing crisis was fuelled by an equally strong illusion: that house values would continue to rise. By the early 2000s, real estate had become the beating heart of the American Dream, and buying a house was seen as a safe investment. Between 2000 and 2006, the median US house price increased by about 50%, with prices in certain places doubling or even tripling. The whole economy seemed to revolve around housing, with mortgage-backed securities (MBS) transforming subprime loans into 'safe' investments and Wall Street packaging them into profitable assets. It was a system based on collective overconfidence, in which every participant—from lenders and purchasers to investors—believed they were part of a flawless market.

But behind this covering of affluence, an unsteady foundation was emerging. Banks started lending without regard for creditworthiness, tempting customers with promises of adjustable-rate mortgages, zero-down choices, and 'interest-only' payments. By 2006, almost 20% of all new mortgages were subprime, meaning they were issued to people with dubious credit. These subprime loans were packaged into mortgage-backed securities and marketed to investors all over the globe who were drawn to the supposedly low-risk, high-reward appeal of American real estate. Between 2003 and 2007, banks issued approximately $1.3 trillion in subprime mortgages, resulting in a web of linked risk that spanned the entire financial system. Nonetheless, the inefficiency was concealed by growing prices, uncontrolled optimism, and the notion that property values were impervious to economic downturns.

When property prices peaked in 2006 and began to fall, the whole structure began to deteriorate. By the middle of 2007, subprime mortgage defaults were skyrocketing, leaving banks with billions of dollars in losses as foreclosures piled up. Lehman Brothers, a banking giant with $600 billion in assets mainly connected to mortgage-backed securities, fell in September 2008, sending shockwaves across the global economy. The domino effect was devastating: mortgage defaults skyrocketed, banks stopped lending, and stock markets plunged. Between October 2007 and March 2009, the S&P 500 lost roughly 57% of its value, wiping away more than $7 trillion in shareholder capital (Malmendier & Nagel, 2011). Unemployment skyrocketed as industries closed, plunging the country into a severe recession.

These subprime loans were central to the financial system's growing instability. Banks, driven by the potential for high returns, packaged these risky loans into mortgage-backed securities (MBS) and sold them to investors worldwide. Investment banks further transformed these securities into complex financial products like collateralised debt obligations (CDOs), which were given high credit ratings by rating agencies despite their underlying risks. Between 2003 and 2007, approximately $1.3 trillion in subprime mortgages were issued, creating an interconnected web of financial risk. These securities were marketed as low-risk, high-reward investments, underpinned by the flawed assumption that housing prices would never decline.

However, the foundations of this system were inherently unstable. The reliance on continuously rising property values masked the underlying inefficiencies and risks. Many subprime borrowers faced unsustainable debt levels, particularly as adjustable-rate mortgages began resetting to higher interest rates. By 2006, housing prices began to peak and then decline, setting off a cascade of financial failures. Borrowers defaulted on their loans at alarming rates, triggering massive losses for financial institutions holding or trading mortgage-backed securities.

The crisis reached its apex in September 2008 with the collapse of Lehman Brothers, one of the largest investment banks in the United States. With $600 billion in assets, much of it tied to mortgage-backed securities, Lehman Brothers' bankruptcy was the largest in US history and sent shockwaves throughout the global financial system. The failure of Lehman Brothers exposed the deep vulnerabilities within the financial sector, leading to a loss of confidence in banks and credit markets. Interbank lending froze, liquidity evaporated, and major financial institutions faced insolvency, necessitating government intervention on an unprecedented scale.

The economic repercussions were devastating. Between October 2007 and March 2009, the S&P 500 lost approximately 57% of its value, erasing over $7 trillion in shareholder wealth. Unemployment in the United States soared, reaching 10% by October 2009, with over 8.7 million jobs lost during the recession. Entire industries, particularly construction and manufacturing, collapsed as credit dried up and demand plummeted. Foreclosures surged, with approximately 3 million households losing their homes between 2007 and 2010. The crisis quickly spread globally, triggering recessions in Europe, Asia, and emerging markets as the interconnected financial system transmitted the shockwaves worldwide.

Government responses to the crisis included significant fiscal and monetary interventions. In the United States, the Troubled Asset Relief Program (TARP) authorised $700 billion to stabilise the financial sector by purchasing toxic assets and injecting capital into struggling banks. The Federal Reserve slashed interest rates to near zero and implemented quantitative easing to restore liquidity and confidence in financial markets (Loang, 2024). Globally, central banks coordinated to provide emergency liquidity and prevent the collapse of critical financial institutions.

The 2008 housing crisis exposed profound flaws in the financial system, including inadequate regulation, excessive risk-taking, and misaligned incentives. Rating agencies, for example, faced scrutiny for granting high ratings to subprime-backed securities, while banks were criticised for prioritising short-term profits over long-term stability. The crisis also revealed the dangers of over-leveraging, as financial institutions operated with thin capital buffers that left them vulnerable to shocks.

In the aftermath, policymakers introduced sweeping reforms to address these systemic issues. The Dodd-Frank Wall Street Reform and Consumer Protection Act of 2010 introduced stricter regulations on financial institutions, increased transparency in derivatives markets, and created the Consumer Financial Protection Bureau (CFPB) to protect borrowers. However, debates continue over the effectiveness of these measures and the potential for new financial crises.

The 2008 housing crisis remains a cautionary tale of overconfidence, systemic risk, and the dangers of speculative bubbles. It underscores the importance of robust financial regulation, transparency, and a focus on sustainability over short-term gains (Hirshleifer, 2015). As financial markets evolve, the lessons of 2008 serve as a reminder of the catastrophic consequences when risk is mispriced, and the collective belief in infallibility eclipses reality.

The 2008 crisis was more than simply a downturn; it was a painful reminder of the consequences of unrestrained market inefficiency. Housing, previously seen as the foundation of financial stability, has become the epicentre of global economic instability. The crisis highlighted vulnerabilities in a system that prioritised short-term profits above long-term stability, demonstrating the capacity of market inefficiencies to transform whole economies. As prices collapsed, millions' dreams of prosperity via homeownership became nightmares, highlighting the hazards of a market fuelled by speculation and without a solid foundation. The financial world was forever changed, and the crisis served as a sharp reminder of how rapidly market inefficiencies can transform wealth into tragedy.

2.3 Meme Stock Mania of 2021

Few occurrences in contemporary financial history have captivated public interest and challenged traditional beliefs as much as the meme stock phenomena of 2021. What started as informal Internet discourse among novice traders rapidly evolved into a significant movement that profoundly impacted Wall Street. This remarkable episode centred on beleaguered companies such as GameStop and AMC Entertainment, whose stock prices surged to unprecedented levels, not due to financial fundamentals but as a result of collective action driven by social media, discontent with financial inequality, and the democratisation of trading platforms.

The GameStop tale, a conventional video game shop confronting diminishing significance in the digital era, exemplified this approach. By late 2020, hedge funds had significantly shorted GameStop, anticipating a decline in its stock price due to the company's dismal prospects. Short sellers such as Melvin Capital have established substantial holdings, certain that the market would mirror the company's declining financial outlook. A burgeoning cohort of retail traders on the Reddit community WallStreetBets saw an opportunity to challenge the prevailing norms. The traders saw that the significant short interest in GameStop's stock rendered it susceptible to a short squeeze, when escalating prices compel short sellers to repurchase shares to cover their holdings, so unintentionally propelling prices further higher.

This tactic depended not on the inherent worth of GameStop but on the efficacy of collective action. Retail investors, many with no past investment expertise, started aggregating their resources to purchase GameStop shares en masse, propelling the company from under \$20 in early January 2021 to an extraordinary \$483 by the month's conclusion. This 2400% surge in value within a few of weeks contradicted all established financial principles. For several participants, the financial gains were subordinate to the emblematic act of confronting institutional entities that they saw had historically exploited markets for their benefit. On social media, GameStop transcended its status as a mere stock; it became as a rallying cry for the 'little guy' in a struggle against the perceived inequities of Wall Street.

Behavioral finance provides a robust framework for comprehending this phenomena. The herd mentality was apparent as thousands of retail traders, influenced by viral articles and memes, participated in the movement, often without comprehending the associated dangers. Many participants were seized by the fear of missing out as they saw others posting remarkable profits. Social proof—the psychological phenomenon in which people emulate the behaviours of others—intensified the purchasing frenzy, especially when WallStreetBets tweets lauding success stories received thousands of likes and shares. Traders who were originally reluctant were engulfed by the frenzy, convinced that if several others were reaping profits, they too could not afford to be excluded.

A significant factor was confirmation bias, when individuals preferentially concentrated on information that reinforced the idea in the perpetual increase of GameStop's price. Posts on WallStreetBets often highlighted optimistic themes, such the company's prospects for a resurgence or speculative interest from technology investors, while disregarding cautions from experts and sceptics. This selective attention created an echo chamber that promoted favourable feeling while suppressing dissident voices.

The influence of contemporary technologies exacerbated the chaos. Commission-free trading services such as Robinhood enabled beginner investors to effortlessly enter financial markets with little capital. The democratisation of trading reduced entrance barriers, allowing millions of regular investors to engage in the stock market for the first time. Nonetheless, some platforms have also gamified investing by including elements such as confetti animations for transactions and push alerts to promote regular engagement. The outcome was an atmosphere in which trading resembled a video game rather than a serious financial pursuit, hence exacerbating impulsive and speculative behaviour.

As the frenzy peaked, the consequences reflected beyond ordinary investors. Hedge funds with substantial short holdings incurred devastating losses. Melvin cash, a leading short-selling firm, allegedly incurred billions in losses within weeks, necessitating emergency cash infusions. The extraordinary volatility attracted the attention of regulators, lawmakers, and financial institutions globally. Robinhood, encountering liquidity challenges, controversially limited trading on GameStop and other meme stocks, inciting uproar among ordinary traders who saw the action as cooperation with Wall Street to safeguard institutional interests. The limits provoked significant criticism, with legislators and activists demanding more openness and equity in financial markets.

The subsequent collapse of GameStop's stock price was as spectacular as its rise. By February 2021, the price had dropped below $50, erasing a significant portion of the paper riches amassed by latecomers to the speculation. A multitude of retail traders who purchased at the zenith incurred significant losses, while a lucky few who divested early reaped transformative profits. The aftermath highlighted the dangers of speculative investment, especially when motivated by emotion rather than rational thought.

The meme stock phenomena transcended a simple narrative of winners and losers; it was a significant cultural event that transformed the dynamics between individual investors and financial markets. It revealed the weaknesses of a system that had consistently favoured institutional entities while concurrently emphasising the efficacy of collective action in the digital era. For financial theorists, it highlighted the inadequacies of conventional models in elucidating market behaviour influenced by emotion, social dynamics, and technical advancements.

The meme stock phenomenon has prompted significant enquiries over the future of market regulation. Should platforms such as Robinhood be permitted to limit trading during times of significant volatility? How can regulators reconcile the need of safeguarding retail investors from their own decisions while maintaining their entitlement to engage freely in the market? What lessons may financial institutions derive from the disruptive influence of social media and retail activism? The meme stock phenomenon of 2021 was not only a financial oddity; it was a social and psychological occurrence that questioned the fundamental principles of contemporary finance. It illustrated that markets are influenced not just by objective calculations but also by the aspirations, anxieties, and collective mentality of its members. The events involving GameStop and AMC, whether seen as a populist insurrection or a cautionary narrative, will likely provide a substantial subject for analysis in the years ahead, highlighting the erratic interaction between human behaviour and financial markets.

2.4 Silver Squeeze of 1980

The story of the Hunt brothers' attempt to monopolise the silver market in the late 1970s and early 1980s serves as a cautionary tale of unfettered ambition, market manipulation, and the pitfalls of overconfidence. The incident was a massive spectacle involving billions of dollars, tremendous price fluctuation, and a calamitous collapse that shook global financial markets. The episode shows the fragility of speculative bubbles while also clearly illustrating behavioral biases, institutional vulnerabilities, and the perennial human tendency to overestimate control over complex systems.

Nelson Bunker Hunt and William Herbert Hunt, who inherited one of America's largest oil fortunes, began buying silver in the mid-1970s. The Hunts, first spurred by fears about inflation reducing their wealth, regarded silver as a safe-haven asset, similar to gold, during economic downturns. What began as a defensive strategy quickly evolved into a daring attempt to dominate the global silver market. By 1979, the Hunt brothers had amassed an incredible amount of silver—roughly one-third of the world's privately held supply—via a combination of direct buys and futures contracts.

Their operations prompted silver prices to skyrocket. Beginning at about $10 per ounce in early 1979, silver skyrocketed to an incredible $50 per ounce by January 1980, signifying a 400% increase in only 1 year. This astonishing price variation was fuelled not by a rise in industrial demand or a supply interruption but by the Hunts' ongoing purchase efforts, which sparked speculation from other investors looking to profit on the trend. As prices soared, the Hunts' confidence grew, bolstering their belief that they could manipulate the market to their benefit. The situation highlighted overconfidence bias, in which individuals overestimate their ability to affect outcomes while overlooking rising hazards and opposing forces.

The rising silver prices have attracted opportunistic investors, aggravating the bubble via herd behaviour. As the Hunts accumulated silver, others, fearful of losing out on prospective riches, followed in, increasing price inflation. This speculative purchase frenzy created a feedback cycle in which rising prices prompted further buys that were completely unrelated to the metal's basic value. According to behavioural finance, this is a sign of positive reinforcement bias, in which short-term earnings justify erroneous decisions, hence perpetuating an overvaluation loop.

However, the same factors that drove silver's fast rise also laid the groundwork for its collapse. As prices rose, market officials became increasingly worried. In

January 1980, the Commodity Exchange (COMEX) and the Chicago Board of Trade (CBOT) implemented more rigorous margin requirements, raising the cost of maintaining large positions in silver futures. This move caused a significant blow to the Hunts, who had heavily leveraged their holdings. Faced with unmanageable margin calls, the brothers were forced to liquidate certain assets, resulting in a dramatic drop in silver prices.

The ensuing events were a financial calamity. Silver prices fell from $50 per ounce to about $11 in 3 months, wiping off billions of dollars in market capitalisation. The Hunts were on the verge of bankruptcy after accumulating significant debt to sustain their positions. Their riches, once among the most considerable in the United States, was destroyed. This stunning drop highlights the illusion of power, as investors believe they can control markets indefinitely while underestimating the complexities and durability of the whole system.

The crash exposed the flaws in the whole financial system. Numerous banks and broking firms that had financed the Hunts' silver buys suffered significant losses, raising concerns about systemic risk. The episode demonstrated the dangers of excessive leverage and the interconnection of financial institutions, foreshadowing subsequent tragedies such as the subprime mortgage crisis almost three decades later.

The dynamics of the silver crunch highlight the combination of greed, dread, and hubris. The Hunts' belief in their ability to manage the silver market masked their sight of rising risks, while the speculative frenzy they instilled in other investors fuelled an unstable bubble. Regulatory efforts, although necessary, were too late to prevent the consequences, demonstrating the challenges of restraining market exuberance in real time.

The silver squeeze of 1980 is a notable case study in speculative bubbles and behavioural finance in financial markets. It demonstrates how biased and emotional decision-making may lead to severe market inefficiencies. The anecdote serves as a sharp warning of the consequences of unfettered ambition, as well as the need of humility while dealing with complex market forces. Since then, the Hunt brothers' story has served as a warning to both investors and authorities. It demonstrates the dangers of overconfidence, the disruptive effects of herd behaviour, and the critical necessity for structural safeguards to prevent repeated disasters. Finally, the silver squeeze was not just a financial disaster but also a valuable lesson on the limitations of control and the persistent unpredictability of human behaviour in markets.

2.5 Chinese P2P Lending Crisis (2018–2019)

The development and collapse of China's peer-to-peer (P2P) lending business are a spectacular and frightening story of uncontrolled financial innovation, unrestrained greed, and the destructive effects of behavioural biases at both the individual and institutional levels. At its height, the P2P lending industry represented a beacon of hope for millions of borrowers and investors in China, offering quick loan access and large profits in an environment where conventional banking services often failed to satisfy the requirements of disadvantaged communities. However, by 2019, this once-promising business had almost collapsed, leaving millions of investors with enormous losses and revealing the perils of an unregulated financial system.

The peer-to-peer lending sector began in China in the mid-2000s, owing to the fast digitalisation of financial services and the growth of fintech platforms. Unlike conventional banks, P2P platforms work directly between individual borrowers and lenders, eliminating the need for middlemen. This invention was especially enticing in China, where many small firms and rural communities had difficulty obtaining loans from state-owned banks, which prioritised huge corporations and government-backed projects. For borrowers, P2P networks offered quick access to loans with no paperwork. For lenders, they presented an appealing proposition: yields of 10% or more per year, greatly above the interest rates given by typical savings accounts.

Behavioural biases played an important influence in the industry's rapid rise. The availability heuristic was especially visible, as platforms promoted instances of regular people attaining financial success via peer-to-peer lending. These experiences, along with strong marketing initiatives, contributed to the idea that peer-to-peer lending was a low-risk, high-reward proposition. Investors often overlooked the underlying hazards, instead focussing on the compelling success tales that dominated public debate. This selective focus on good results, along with the overconfidence bias, caused many to assume they could safely manage the market and maximise their gains without fully comprehending the complexity involved.

By 2015, China's peer-to-peer lending business was witnessing exponential expansion. The number of platforms increased to almost 6000, and the total transaction volume surpassed 1 trillion yuan. However, underneath this fast development were a number of systemic weaknesses. Many platforms operated with little to no monitoring, taking advantage of legislative gaps to engage in risky behaviour. Some platforms offered guaranteed profits, an obvious breach of financial rules, while others utilised cash from new investors to repay previous ones—a typical Ponzi scheme structure. The absence of openness and due diligence on both sides of the market produced a climate conducive to exploitation.

Herd behaviour aggravated the problem. As the business grew in prominence, more investors gravitated to P2P networks, motivated by the fear of missing out. The greater the rewards promised by a platform, the more investors it drew, regardless of the platform's legitimacy or financial strength. Social proof was important in this case, since individuals were soothed by the large number of participants and the image of legitimacy offered by slick marketing efforts and celebrity endorsements.

The government's early attitude on peer-to-peer lending helped to the industry's unrestricted expansion. Seeing the industry as a way to promote financial inclusion and entrepreneurship, authorities took a hands-off attitude, allowing platforms to operate with little oversight. However, as the sector grew, flaws started to develop. By 2016, allegations of defaults and fraudulent schemes had become more widespread. In other situations, platform operators vanished with investors' money, leaving no record and no recourse for victims. These instances were not isolated; they were part of a larger pattern of systematic abuse made possible by a lack of monitoring.

The turning point occurred in 2018, when the Chinese government, frightened by the extent of the issue, launched a broad assault on the peer-to-peer lending business. Regulatory authorities imposed stronger compliance standards, requiring platforms to declare their financial operations and register with local governments. These steps, although essential, resulted in a massive exit of platforms from the market. Many smaller operations, unable or unable to fulfil the new criteria, closed overnight, taking investors' money with them. By 2019, over 5000 systems had failed, and transaction volume had fallen. The once-thriving industry was essentially eliminated.

The crisis has far-reaching consequences. Millions of investors, including middle-class families and pensioners, experienced substantial financial losses. For others, the collapse of P2P networks meant the loss of life savings, putting them into financial difficulties. The social effects were as severe. Protests broke out in major cities, with disgruntled investors demanding justice and government involvement. These protests underlined the human cost of financial innovation gone awry, as well as the profound feeling of betrayal felt by individuals who had put their faith in a system that eventually failed them.

From a behavioural finance standpoint, the P2P loan crisis highlights the pitfalls of overreaction and confirmation bias in financial decision-making. During the industry's peak years, investors tended to overestimate the safety and profitability of P2P platforms, ignoring warning indications in favour of narratives that reinforced their confidence. This prejudice was exacerbated by the platforms' aggressive marketing techniques, which painted a distorted picture of the risks and benefits involved. When the bubble broke, the pendulum swung the other way, with investors quitting even respectable platforms in a wave of panic selling and suspicion.

The crisis has also highlighted the value of regulatory monitoring in minimising systemic risks. The lack of defined regulations and enforcement methods enabled unscrupulous actors to take advantage of the system, undermining faith in the whole sector. While the government's crackdown did eventually bring the issue under control, it was too late to avert huge losses and long-term harm to the sector's image.

In hindsight, the peer-to-peer lending crisis serves as a warning tale about the dangers of financial innovation without sufficient oversight. It demonstrates how behavioural biases may fuel unsustainable growth, resulting in bubbles that ultimately implode. It also emphasises the need of regulation in balancing innovation and stability, safeguarding both investors and the whole financial system. For China, the crisis taught a painful but crucial lesson about the dangers of unfettered markets. It led politicians to reconsider their approach to fintech and financial inclusion, resulting in tighter regulation of online lending platforms and a greater focus on investor education. For the global financial community, it serves as a warning that, although technology might democratise access to money, it also creates new dangers that must be managed with caution. The P2P lending disaster was more than simply a failure of legislation or business ethics; it was also a failure to account for market players' complicated and frequently illogical behaviour, a lesson that has far-reaching consequences beyond China's borders.

References

An, L., Wang, H., Wang, J., & Yu, J. (2020). Lottery-related anomalies: The role of reference-dependent preferences. *Management Science, 66*(1), 473–501.

Barberis, N., & Thaler, R. (2003). A survey of behavioral finance. In G. M. Constantinides, M. Harris, & R. M. Stulz (Eds.), *Handbook of the economics of finance* (Vol. 1, pp. 1053–1128). Elsevier.

Ben-David, I., Graham, J. R., & Harvey, C. R. (2013). Managerial miscalibration. *The Quarterly Journal of Economics, 128*(4), 1547–1584.

Coval, J. D., & Shumway, T. (2005). Do behavioral biases affect prices? *The Journal of Finance, 60*(1), 1–34.

Gervais, S., & Odean, T. (2001). Learning to be overconfident. *The Review of Financial Studies, 14*(1), 1–27.

Hirshleifer, D. (2015). Behavioral finance. *Annual Review of Financial Economics, 7*(1), 133–159.

Kumar, A. (2009). Who gambles in the stock market? *The Journal of Finance, 64*(4), 1889–1933.

Lo, A. W. (2004). The adaptive markets hypothesis: Market efficiency from an evolutionary perspective. *Journal of Portfolio Management, Forthcoming.*

Loang, O. K. (2024). Financial stability at risk: Evidence from market overreaction and herding behaviour in developed and emerging markets. *China Finance Review International.*

Malmendier, U., & Nagel, S. (2011). Depression babies: Do macroeconomic experiences affect risk taking? *The Quarterly Journal of Economics, 126*(1), 373–416.

Statman, M. (2017). *Finance for normal people: How investors and markets behave*. Oxford University Press.

Chapter 3
Behavioral Finance and Traditional Finance

For decades, finance was seen as a science of certainties and systems, in which mathematical models seemed to encapsulate investor behaviour and anticipate market swings. At the centre of this viewpoint was the EMH, an elegant theory championed by Eugene Fama at the University of Chicago in the 1960s (Huberman, 2001). According to EMH, markets absorbed all available information instantly. Hence, stock prices always represent genuine worth. What is the logical conclusion? Outperforming the market was almost impossible. According to this approach, beating the market was a gamble—a fool's errand. Investors were supposed to be rational actors who calculated risk and maximised profits based only on facts and reasoning.

This concept became the foundation of conventional finance and expanded to colleges, investment businesses, and economic policy talks. Students discovered that markets were practically faultless, functioning with accuracy and fairness. To EMH experts, the concept of 'market inefficiencies' was ridiculous. If anomalies arose, such as unexpected price spikes or falls, they were seen as minor blips in an otherwise perfect system. EMH maintained that these temporary disturbances were just statistical noise that rational market participants would rapidly remedy.

However, in the 1970s, a new generation of researchers started to see patterns that EMH failed to explain. Researchers noted occurrences such as the January effect, in which small-cap stocks fared very well in January, and the momentum effect, in which stocks that had previously gained continued to increase while those that had declined fell more. These unusual, reoccurring behaviours could not be readily discounted. If markets were entirely efficient, why would these patterns persist? While EMH proponents dismissed them as statistical anomalies, a few intellectuals started to wonder whether markets—and the people who inhabit them—were genuinely rational.

Initially, these sceptics encountered pushback. The notion of rational markets was well ingrained in academia, and challenging EMH meant challenging decades of work. Fama and his colleagues stood firm, claiming that irregularities were

K. L. Ooi, *Demystifying Behavioral Finance*,
https://doi.org/10.1007/978-981-96-2690-8_3

immaterial in the broader scheme of finance. But when unusual patterns emerged, the scene was prepared for a paradigm shift in economic thinking. Scholars from various disciplines, like psychologists, sociologists, and historians, began to examine finance and ask whether conventional models were missing something essential about human nature (Thaler & Sunstein, 2008).

Daniel Kahneman and Amos Tversky first met in the early 1970s, kicking off a relationship that would call into question some of economics and finance's most basic assumptions. Despite being trained as psychologists, Kahneman and Tversky had little prior experience with market theory. They were more interested in how individuals made choices in the face of uncertainty than in stock prices or asset returns. What they discovered was shocking: individuals often made irrational decisions, succumbing to a variety of cognitive biases and psychological quirks.

Kahneman and Tversky conducted years of tests that demonstrated how people used mental shortcuts, or heuristics, to make complex judgements fast. While these heuristics helped individuals manage an overwhelming universe of options, they also resulted in predictable blunders. In one landmark experiment, they discovered that individuals employed anchoring—making judgements based on a single piece of information, even if it was arbitrary. When asked to estimate the number of African nations in the United Nations, participants' responses were impacted by a predetermined random number spun on a wheel. The greater the number, the higher their estimations. This 'anchoring' bias would go on to explain why investors could stick to their original view about a stock's worth even if fresh facts showed differently.

Their research on prospect theory would have an even more significant influence on finance. In their influential 1979 work, 'Prospect Theory: An Analysis of Decision under Risk', Kahneman and Tversky demonstrated that people's actions were not motivated by absolute values but rather by profits and losses relative to a benchmark. The idea of loss aversion, which states that the pain of losing $100 is more severe than the pleasure of receiving $100, has become a cornerstone of behavioural economics. Loss aversion explained why investors were often unwilling to sell losing equities, preferring to stay on in the chance of a reversal, even when rationality demanded that they should cut their losses.

Prospect theory proposed that people's fear of loss often surpassed their desire for gain, causing them to make poor financial decisions. This contrasted starkly with EMH, which believed that all investors would act rationally and in their best interests. Kahneman and Tversky contended that human behaviour was more complicated, emotional, and unpredictable than conventional finance recognised.

Their insights paved the way for a new field: behavioural finance. Kahneman and Tversky revealed peculiarities in human psychology and highlighted fundamental problems in economists' understanding of markets. By demonstrating that individuals were consistently irrational, they called into question the basic concept of a 'rational investor' and the premise that markets could ever be completely efficient. Their results echoed across fields and piqued the curiosity of economists, sociologists, and politicians alike.

Kahneman elaborated on these concepts in his 2011 blockbuster *Thinking, Fast and Slow*, which explored the twin systems of the human mind. He identified two types of thinking: System 1, which is quick, intuitive, and prone to mistakes, and System 2, which is slower, more methodical, and more precise. According to Kahneman, System 1 drives the majority of financial decisions, causing investors to make rash and impulsive decisions. *Thinking, Fast and Slow* captured both the academic and popular worlds, introducing behavioural finance concepts to a worldwide audience and emphasising the necessity of understanding human psychology in financial markets (Barber & Odean, 2000).

Despite the pioneering nature of Kahneman and Tversky's research, only some were persuaded. Traditional finance researchers, headed by Eugene Fama, were very sceptical of the notion that markets might be consistently irrational. For Fama and his colleagues, EMH was more than a theory; it was a passionately believed ideology that moulded whole lives. The efficient market hypothesis assumes that any irrational behaviour would be neutralised by rational agents, causing prices to stabilise at actual value. To them, behavioural finance was intriguing but ultimately insignificant—more of an exciting side note than a threat to the fundamental concepts of finance.

Fama contended that although individual investors may behave irrationally, the combined actions of all market players will result in an efficient system. Even if some traders behaved emotionally, he felt that the great majority would make judgements based on available evidence, ensuring that markets remained logical. When behavioural economists pointed out anomalies like as the January effect, which showed that small-cap stocks rose in January, Fama rejected them as statistical oddities. According to him, these benefits evaporated after transaction fees and other practical issues were taken into account.

However, the accumulating amount of data from Kahneman, Tversky, and their allies took a lot of work to ignore. They have established biases that influence practically every investment. Their analysis revealed that investors were not making random errors; instead, they were making the same mistakes again (Ackert & Deaves, 2009). This predictability implied that irrationality was inherent in human behaviour, a systematic force that could not be rectified by the market's 'invisible hand'.

The scholarly debate over conventional and behavioural finance intensified. Conferences became battlegrounds, with economists arguing over the consequences of irrationality. Fama and his colleagues continued to say that anomalies were immaterial in the larger picture of market behaviour, but behavioral economists contended that these patterns revealed EMH's flaws. Each side collected data and created models to support their positions. Still, the debate remained deadlocked until real-world events pushed the financial sector to address the role of investor psychology in markets.

While Kahneman and Tversky established the theoretical framework, Richard Thaler became the public face of behavioural finance. Thaler was attracted by their work, viewing it as a framework for explaining the anomalies he had seen in financial behaviour. He dug further into topics such as mental accounting, which involves treating money differently depending on its source or intended purpose. This resulted in illogical spending and saving practices, such as using a tax return as 'bonus money' to splurge rather than putting it towards long-term savings.

Thaler elaborated on these concepts in his 2008 book, *Nudge: Improving Decisions About Health, Wealth, and Happiness*, which he co-authored with legal expert Cass Sunstein. Thaler proposed the notion of 'nudges' in *Nudge*, which are minor modifications in how options are presented that may lead to improved decisions. One of Thaler's most famous recommendations was automatic enrolment in retirement savings programmes, which took advantage of people's innate predisposition towards inertia. Thaler suggested that making saving the default choice would allow corporations to 'nudge' people towards financially savvy actions without compulsion. *Nudge* was a worldwide triumph, influencing public policy and introducing behavioural economics to the mainstream.

Thaler's 2015 book, *Misbehaving: The Making of Behavioral Economics*, detailed his path from economic outsider to Nobel winner, including conflicts with orthodox economists and difficulties achieving recognition for behavioural finance. In *Misbehaving*, Thaler described how cognitive biases like loss aversion and overconfidence influenced real-world market behaviour, resulting in inefficiencies that previous models could not explain. The book cemented Thaler's position as a transformational figure in economics, and his findings verified Kahneman and Tversky's ideas.

The narrative of behavioural finance is more than simply a few landmark research; it is about a chorus of voices who steadily, and sometimes doggedly, carved out a place for psychology in the world of finance. As behavioural finance gained traction, a new generation of thinkers developed, each offering their distinctive perspective and improving our knowledge of how the human mind influences market.

Hersh Shefrin is one of those voices, a researcher who has bravely revealed the psychological traps that investors fall into. Shefrin and Meir Statman investigated the disposition effect, a peculiar phenomenon in which investors sell winning equities too early and hang onto losing stocks for too long. Why? It is not a logical decision but one motivated by emotions such as pride in accomplishment and a solid unwillingness to concede loss. Shefrin and Statman showed how these emotions influence decision-making, demonstrating that investment is only partially rational. They also looked at mental accounting, a bias in which individuals value money differently based on its origin or planned purpose, even when it contradicts logic. Their work depicted investing as a mental battleground, where pride, anxiety, and even apparently little characteristics of 'how we think' may lead to conclusions that deviate from logic.

Then there's Robert Shiller, a Nobel winner and towering figure in finance, whose studies shed light on how speculative bubbles form and bust. Shiller's book, *Irrational Exuberance*, served as a forewarning of both the dot-com boom and the subsequent housing market crash. His study, published only months before the IT catastrophe, caught the collective craze of markets, demonstrating how investors, intoxicated by soaring prices and each other's enthusiasm, generate catastrophic feedback loops that drive prices well beyond their inherent worth. Shiller claimed that prices are more than simply numbers; they are representations of tales, hope, and the exhilarating but risky notion that 'this time it's different'. Shiller's work demonstrated that markets are social creatures, alive with their members' expectations and fears—a viewpoint that reshaped our understanding of asset bubbles and market volatility (Kumar, 2009).

Finally, Terrance Odean focused on the individual investor's mindset, highlighting the risks and advantages of overconfidence. Odean's research revealed the layers of frequent traders who, sometimes filled with misguided confidence, trade more than they should, confident they have an advantage. However, Odean's study revealed a grim truth: these overconfident investors often fared worse than their more cautious counterparts, draining profits due to excessive trading and lousy timing. Odean discovered, in collaboration with Brad Barber, that overconfidence was not simply a harmless characteristic; it was also financially harmful, reducing earnings and multiplying risks. His research indicated that our predisposition to feel we are 'smarter than the market' may be our downfall, a message that continues to resonate with investors and advisers today. Together, these researchers created a story of finance that was no longer clean and faultless but somewhat human, messy, and highly psychological. Their research transformed behavioural finance from a minor interest to a formidable foundation for understanding the brains that drive markets.

3.1 Black Monday: When Panic Overrides Rationality

One of the most spectacular instances of behavioural finance at work occurred on October 19, 1987—a day that would become known as Black Monday. On that day, the Dow Jones Industrial Average fell by a whopping 22.6% in a single session, the market's most significant single-day percentage decrease ever. The financial world was left reeling; nothing in standard finance theory could explain such a dramatic and unexpected decline. There were no cataclysmic news events or economic indications pointing to an impending disaster—only a sudden, incomprehensible wave of dread that grabbed investors throughout the world.

Behavioural finance researchers cited Black Monday as a prime example of herd behaviour. In times of uncertainty, individuals often rely on the acts of others to influence their judgements. When investors observed others selling, a feeling of urgency developed, prompting an increasing number of individuals to join the sell-off. This widespread fear triggered a feedback cycle, escalating the initial price decline into a full-fledged collapse. Kahneman and Tversky's research on loss aversion shed further light on why the response was so strong. Investors were not just worried about their holdings; they were frightened of losing everything. Loss aversion heightened their dread, forcing them to sell at any price in order to avoid future drops.

Furthermore, mental shortcuts, often known as heuristics, contributed significantly to the severity of Black Monday. One of the most influential was the

3.3 Days of the Week Effect

The 'days of the week effect' is a unique and long-standing behavioural finance anomaly that calls into question the foundations of rational and efficient markets. It refers to identifiable patterns in stock market returns that vary frequently depending on the day of the week. Although traditional financial theories suggest that market returns should be random and unrelated to the calendar, empirical evidence repeatedly contradicts this view. For decades, researchers have observed that stock markets tend to have lower or negative returns on Mondays and higher returns on Fridays, among other tendencies. These abnormalities are deeply ingrained in market participants' psychological biases and emotional dispositions, giving a unique glimpse into the human side of finance.

The days of the week effect is basically based on investor mood, which fluctuates owing to a combination of psychological, social, and cultural factors. Mondays, sometimes known as 'blue Mondays', show lower returns across several global markets. This trend is sometimes attributed to the mood theory, which says that unpleasant feeling at the start of the workweek, caused by the shift from the weekend, influences trading conduct. Investors may start Monday with a more pessimistic outlook, resulting in increased selling pressure and a drop in market performance. Fridays, on the other hand, are often associated with good moods and the prospect of a weekend, resulting in more risk-taking and bigger price variations.

Empirical research backs up these conclusions. French (1980) conducted important research on the Monday impact in US stock markets, indicating that returns on Mondays were much lower than on other days. Subsequent research has corroborated this pattern across worldwide markets, demonstrating that it is not exclusive to a certain geographic or cultural situation. Research on European and Asian markets has shown similar day-of-the-week tendencies, with Mondays consistently underperforming and Fridays producing higher returns.

Although sentiment and mood offer a compelling explanation for the days of the week effect, behavioural finance sheds more light on the underlying mechanisms. A critical component is loss aversion, which is a key facet of prospect theory. Investors are more sensitive to losses than gains, a trend that frequently worsens at the start of the week when markets restart operations following the weekend. Negative news that build over the weekend may have a disproportionate impact on trading decisions on Mondays, resulting in risk-averse behaviour and downward price pressure. Conversely, as the week progresses, optimism frequently rises, peaking on Fridays when investors demonstrate increased confidence and a larger proclivity for risk-taking.

The overconfidence bias plays a crucial role in explaining Friday optimism. As the trading week finishes, investors may overestimate their ability to foresee market volatility or the strength of their holdings, leading in increased purchase activity. This overconfidence may result in a feedback loop, since raising rates on Fridays reinforces a positive mindset and encourages additional involvement.

Cultural and institutional factors can impact the days of the week effect. In countries with shorter business hours or where weekends are culturally significant, the Monday influence may be more pronounced. Furthermore, institutional investors, who have a large impact on market dynamics, often execute trades early in the week based on weekend study. This increased activity may exacerbate negative pressure on Mondays, although retail investor enthusiasm later in the week may add to the Friday effect.

Despite its longevity, the Days of the Week Effect has been subject to criticism and scrutiny, particularly in light of changing economics and technological advancements. Sceptics argue that these anomalies will fade over time as markets grow more efficient and computerised trading reduces human biases. Nonetheless, although the severity of the effect may have decreased in certain markets, it has not fully disappeared. Behavioural biases are deeply ingrained in human psychology and continue to influence decision-making, hence the days of the week effect is relevant in today's financial situation.

Furthermore, recent research shows that, although the Monday effect has lessened in many established markets, it remains considerable in emerging countries, where individual investors wield more power and market dynamics are more susceptible to sentiment-driven trading. Research on Asian markets, notably in India and China, frequently finds significant day-of-week tendencies, implying that cultural and structural differences contribute to the longevity of these anomalies.

The days of the week effect provides investors with both opportunities and hurdles. Understanding these trends may assist guide trading strategies, such as when to buy or sell to coincide with profitable days. For example, contrarian investors may benefit from the Monday effect by purchasing shares at lower prices after a weekend-induced slump, while momentum traders may benefit from the Friday effect by capitalising on the current optimism. Nonetheless, these strategies need a thorough examination of transaction costs, liquidity, and market-specific dynamics, since the potential advantages of capitalising on these anomalies may be outweighed by other factors.

The days of the week effect demonstrates the limitations of standard finance theories in explaining real market action. It emphasises the importance of psychology, mood, and cultural factors in affecting financial outcomes, refuting the concept that markets function only on logical principles. Understanding the behavioural drivers of this anomaly provides crucial insights for researchers, policymakers, and practitioners into the complexities of market dynamics and the long-term consequences of human conduct. The days of the week effect is more than just statistical curiosity; it serves as a powerful reminder of the human component in finance. It highlights how, despite technological advancements and increased market complexity, emotionally and psychologically driven patterns continue to affect market conduct. As long as human actors shape markets, the interaction of mood, sentiment, and cognitive biases will continue to produce intriguing anomalies like the days of the week effect, posing both challenges and opportunities for those attempting to understand and navigate the dynamic realm of finance.

3.4 The Monday Effect: A Weekly Reminder of Emotional Impact

Another puzzling phenomenon that behavioural finance attempted to explain was the Monday effect—the propensity for equities to underperform on Mondays relative to other days of the week. Traditional finance failed to explain this trend since there was no logical reason why Mondays should continuously perform worse than Tuesdays or Thursdays. EMH would argue that each trading day should be treated independently of the others, with pricing based only on available information rather than the day of the week.

Behavioural finance researchers claimed that the Monday effect was caused by investor emotions and emotional carry-over from the previous weekend. Weekends allowed investors to process the news, and without the ability to trade, fears typically grew. By Monday, those fears had grown, resulting in a more cautious, even gloomy market environment. Investors who were stewing over unpleasant news or pondering on personal fears were more inclined to sell on Monday mornings, putting downward pressure on prices.

At first glance, the idea that markets could behave differently on specific days seems counterintuitive. What makes Monday so special? The answer lies in the interplay between human emotions, weekend breaks, and the unique rhythm of market activity. Weekends, far from being neutral time-off periods, serve as a psychological buffer where investors have the chance to reflect, analyse, and—crucially—ruminate. Without the distraction of real-time trading, fears and anxieties often fester. A piece of bad news that might have been shrugged off during a busy trading day suddenly looms larger when given the space of two quiet days to grow (Thaler & Sunstein, 2008). By the time Monday arrives, these amplified concerns manifest as cautious or bearish trading behaviour.

Behavioural finance offers profound insights into the emotional underpinnings of the Monday effect. Unlike traditional models that treat investors as rational agents, behavioural theories recognise that moods and emotions heavily influence decision-making. For many investors, weekends act as an emotional reset, temporarily distancing them from the pressures of the market. Returning to the trading floor or portfolio management on Monday often brings a confrontation with unresolved fears, whether personal or financial. This emotional weight often translates into a more pessimistic outlook, prompting sell-offs or risk-averse trading that puts downward pressure on equity prices.

Richard Thaler's work on mental accounting adds another layer of depth to the phenomenon. Thaler theorised that people mentally compartmentalise their experiences, creating distinct 'accounts' for different aspects of life. Weekends, for instance, are often placed in a separate mental account from the workweek. During this time, investors may feel temporarily insulated from financial stress, allowing them to relax. But when the market reopens on Monday, the mental account shifts abruptly, forcing them to reconcile their personal feelings with the financial realities of the week ahead. This transition can be jarring, particularly if unresolved anxieties from the weekend resurface, leading to more cautious or defensive trading behaviour.

The Monday effect also reflects a broader trend of mood contagion within financial markets. Markets are not simply collections of isolated investors acting independently; they are ecosystems of interconnected participants whose emotions and decisions influence one another. If a significant portion of traders enters the market with a bearish outlook on Monday, it creates a feedback loop, reinforcing negative sentiment across the board. This collective caution snowballs into a phenomenon large enough to impact market performance, further fuelling the perception of Mondays as 'bad days' for equities.

Empirical evidence supports the existence of the Monday effect, though its magnitude has varied over time and across markets. Studies have consistently shown that average returns on Mondays tend to be lower compared to other weekdays, particularly in small-cap and less liquid stocks, which are more susceptible to the emotional decisions of retail investors. Some research even suggests that the Monday effect is most pronounced following weekends with negative news events, reinforcing the idea that emotional carry-over plays a central role.

The Monday effect is not merely an academic curiosity—it has practical implications for traders, portfolio managers, and behavioural economists. For active traders, understanding the emotional tendencies that drive Monday trading can provide a strategic edge. For example, if Monday mornings are prone to sell-offs due to emotional pessimism, they may present buying opportunities for those with a more measured approach. Similarly, for behavioural economists, the Monday effect underscores the importance of mood and timing in financial decision-making, offering further evidence that markets are far from purely rational.

Despite its persistence, the Monday effect has waned in recent years, largely due to the rise of algorithmic trading and the globalisation of financial markets. Automated systems are unaffected by human emotions and are less likely to perpetuate psychological biases, while global trading ensures that news flows continuously, reducing the reflective pause traditionally associated with weekends. Nevertheless, remnants of the Monday effect remain, particularly in smaller markets or among individual investors, demonstrating that human psychology still holds sway in certain corners of the financial world (Laibson, 1997).

Thaler's discoveries on mental accounting added depth to this idea. People prefer to categorise their experiences into distinct mental 'accounts', and weekends were a respite from the financial world—a reset. Returning to the market on Monday often meant confronting a mental 'account' of the upcoming week, which might intensify negative sentiments. The Monday effect was more than simply a random trend; it demonstrated how time, mood, and mental compartmentalisation might impact market behaviour, resulting in inefficiencies that orthodox finance could not explain.

3.5 The Halloween Effect: When Superstition and Strategy Collide

The Halloween effect is another market aberration that questions the rational investor hypothesis. This tendency shows that equities perform better between October 31 and May 1 than between May and October—a trend captured by the proverb, 'Sell in May and go away'. Traditional finance theories failed to explain this seasonal impact because there was no fundamental reason why markets should consistently underperform over the summer months.

At first glance, the Halloween effect appears counterintuitive. Why would market performance consistently vary depending on the time of year? Traditional theories argue that asset prices reflect all available information and that seasonal patterns, if widely known, should be arbitraged away. However, the Halloween effect persists, hinting at underlying behavioural forces. Behavioural finance provides a lens to understand this anomaly, revealing how mood, psychological biases, and cultural rhythms intertwine to shape market behaviour.

The months between October and May are often associated with a sense of renewal and optimism, particularly during the holiday season and the start of a new year. Investors, buoyed by the festive atmosphere and the symbolic 'fresh start' of January, often approach the market with increased confidence and risk appetite. This psychological uplift may result in greater willingness to allocate funds to equities, fuelling higher returns during these months. Additionally, institutional investors often adjust their portfolios at year end, contributing to market momentum that carries into the early months of the following year.

In contrast, the summer months, from May to October, are often marked by a lull in market activity. Investors and fund managers are more likely to take vacations, disengage from the market, or focus on personal responsibilities, leading to reduced trading volumes. Lower liquidity during this period can exacerbate volatility and contribute to weaker returns. This seasonal shift in engagement, compounded by a psychological propensity to 'check out' during warmer months, offers a plausible behavioural explanation for the underperformance of equities in summer.

Moreover, the Halloween effect may also be linked to broader psychological phenomena, such as seasonal affective disorder (SAD). SAD, characterised by mood shifts during the darker months of the year, affects risk tolerance and decision-making. While it might seem paradoxical, some studies suggest that the anticipation of colder months—and the associated psychological effects—could lead investors to adopt more conservative investment strategies during the autumn and winter. This aversion to risk might shift capital towards safer assets, inadvertently creating more favourable conditions for equities to rebound during the latter half of the year.

The Halloween effect, like other calendar anomalies, underscores a significant limitation of traditional finance: the assumption that markets are entirely rational and free from human emotion. Patterns like this reveal that markets are, in fact, deeply influenced by the collective psychology of their participants. The idea that market performance could hinge on seasonal mood shifts, cultural practices, or investor disengagement is a powerful reminder of the human element underlying financial systems.

This anomaly is not just a statistical curiosity but a challenge to the efficient market hypothesis. EMH posits that prices fully reflect all available information, leaving no room for predictable patterns. Yet the Halloween effect persists, demonstrating how behavioural tendencies create inefficiencies that defy rational explanations. The enduring nature of this pattern also suggests that psychological and cultural factors are more deeply entrenched in market dynamics than conventional theories acknowledge.

The Halloween effect is not alone in this category of calendar anomalies. Similar patterns, such as the January effect and the Monday effect, further highlight how emotional and psychological factors influence markets in ways that traditional models struggle to explain. Together, these anomalies reveal a broader truth: markets are not purely mechanistic systems governed solely by data and logic. Instead, they are deeply human constructs shaped by emotions, traditions, and biases.

The anomalies discussed—Black Monday, the January effect, the Monday effect, and the Halloween effect—are only a few instances of how real-world market trends contradict established financial theory. Behavioural finance offers a framework for comprehending these repeating events, implying that they are not random occurrences but rather reflections of human nature. Richard Thaler's research on mental accounting, endowment effects, and overconfidence has helped to explain why investors behave in ways that result in seasonal patterns and predictable market inefficiencies.

Each of these anomalies underscores a critical flaw in the EMH: its assumption that investors are rational actors who make decisions purely based on available information. In reality, market participants are deeply influenced by emotions, cognitive biases, and social dynamics. These influences often lead to irrational behaviours, such as panic selling during Black Monday or optimism-fuelled buying during the January effect. The Monday effect highlights the emotional carry-over of weekend worries, while the Halloween effect demonstrates how seasonal mood shifts and disengagement can impact market performance (Liu & Yu, 2024). These patterns persist because they are rooted in deeply ingrained human behaviours that cannot be arbitraged away entirely, even in the presence of sophisticated market participants.

Behavioural finance does more than identify these anomalies; it seeks to explain their resilience. Unlike traditional theories that dismiss such patterns as statistical noise, behavioural finance acknowledges the enduring impact of psychology on financial markets. These anomalies endure because they stem from universal human tendencies—our fear of loss, our inclination to follow the crowd, our susceptibility to mood shifts, and our flawed perceptions of risk. They remind us that markets are not solely governed by data and logic but are shaped by the collective behaviours and emotions of their participants.

3.6 Reversals: Behavioural Anomalies in Market Overreaction

The occurrence of reversals in financial markets, in which previously successful equities (winners) underperform and previously failed stocks (losers) thrive, provides a fascinating glimpse into the psychological roots of market behaviour. Reversals, first observed by De Bondt and Thaler in the 1980s, demonstrate how behavioural irregularities such as overreaction, herd behaviour, and availability bias impact investor decisions, resulting in systematic inefficiencies in stock prices. Contrary to the EMH, these patterns show that human emotions and cognitive biases have a long-term influence on financial markets.

The core of reversals is the phenomenon of overreaction bias, which occurs when investors respond unduly to recent news or events, causing asset prices to diverge significantly from their intrinsic value. When a company experiences positive improvements, such as strong profits growth or favourable market sentiment, investors often overestimate its future potential, inflating its stock price much beyond its fundamental values. In contrast, bad news causes excessive pessimism, which leads to undervaluation. This response is not based on legitimate expectations but rather on a psychological tendency to prioritise present information above historical or contextual aspects.

Empirical data supports the prevalence of reversals, particularly over long timescales. De Bondt and Thaler (1985) observed that portfolios of 'loser' stocks outperformed 'winner' equities by roughly 25% at 3-year intervals. Jegadeesh and Titman (1993) found that equities that performed well for 3–12 months generally saw a turnaround in their trajectory over the next 3–5 years. These tendencies are especially pronounced in speculative and volatile markets, when behavioural biases trump rational reasoning. The dot-com boom of the late 1990s is a prime example. Technology stocks soared as investors, excited by the promise of a 'new economy', ignored profitability indications. Companies like Pets.com had a huge growth in value prior to its collapse in the early 2000s, demonstrating a classic reversal.

The behavioural biases that cause reversals are complicated. One major element is the availability bias, which causes investors to concentrate on recent or conspicuous information. During bull markets, this bias is shown in a fixation with success narratives, such as rising stock prices or noteworthy IPOs, while risks are reduced or ignored. Similarly, confirmation bias exacerbates this problem by encouraging investors to seek information that confirms their optimistic or pessimistic viewpoints, resulting in feedback loops that amplify price differences. During the mid-2000s' housing bubble, tales of ever-increasing property values fuelled a rush of real estate investments, eventually leading to the 2008 financial crisis. The correction in property prices has disastrous consequences, showing the dangers of ignoring fundamental standards.

Herd behaviour is an important factor that influences reversals. Investors often adhere to the majority, believing that group action indicates increased expertise. When a stock's price rises rapidly, others invest, driving prices higher in a speculative frenzy. During downturns, the same herd mentality causes panic selling, lowering prices down below their true value. This dynamic creates opportunities for reversals, as overpriced assets eventually fall and undervalued assets recover. The energy business in 2014 demonstrates this trend. As oil prices plunged from more than $100 per barrel to less than $30, energy stocks—previously preferred by the market—saw huge sell-offs, only to rebound in subsequent years as oil prices steadied.

Critics of the behavioural finance perspective argue that reversals may show risk compensation rather than cognitive mistakes. Underperforming enterprises may have more risks, which may justify their potential for higher earnings as investors seek a risk premium. Similarly, superior-performing shares may see declining returns due to lower risk profiles. However, although this risk-based argument is consistent with traditional financial theories, it fails to account for the psychological and emotional components that emerge during reversal stages. Research shows that even in markets with consistent risk indicators, reversals occur, underscoring the importance of human conduct.

Reversals have significant implications for investment strategies, particularly for contrarian investors seeking to profit from market inefficiencies. Contrarians aim to profit from mean reversion by buying inexpensive stocks and selling overvalued ones, taking advantage of the tendency for significant price movements to stabilise over time. Historical evidence supports the effectiveness of these strategies. Lakonishok et al. (1994) demonstrated that value stocks, often referred to as 'losers', outperformed growth stocks, or 'winners', in the long term. This practice requires patience and discipline, since reversals may take years to show. It also poses significant career risks to fund managers, who may face criticism or capital withdrawals during periods of underperformance.

Despite technology advances and the rise of algorithmic trading, reversals persist owing to their deep roots in human psychology. Algorithms, although intended to decrease human error, often include prior patterns established by behavioural factors, perpetuating the anomalies they want to exploit. Furthermore, behavioural biases such as overreaction, herd behaviour, and loss aversion exist among market participants, confounding the idea of efficient markets via continuous reversals. Reversals are not just a financial anomaly but also a stark reminder of the human side of investing. Cognitive biases and emotional responses impact market dynamics, creating both opportunities and risks for investors. Understanding reversals gives policymakers insights into market irrationality and measures to mitigate it. Reversals underscore the need of integrating behavioural insights into financial theory and practice, providing a more sophisticated view on market conduct. Finally, reversals demonstrate the enduring complexity of human behaviour in financial markets—a complexity that defies simple explanations and continues to enchant both professionals and investors.

3.7 Dogs of the Dow

The 'Dogs of the Dow' concept is a well-known and long-standing investment strategy in the financial markets. Although investing yearly in the Dow Jones Industrial Average's ten top dividend-yielding companies may seem simple, it incorporates more significant behavioural finance ideas that call traditional market efficiency into question. This contrarian approach underscores the long-term impact of behavioural biases on market performance and highlights the potential rewards of disciplined investing while others succumb to psychological traps.

The Dogs of the Dow method is based on identifying and exploiting market inefficiencies caused by investor overreaction and neglect. Firms picked in this technique are often those that have fallen out of favour with the market, resulting in an increased dividend yield when stock prices fall. These 'dogs' are commonly seen as high-risk or underperforming, yet they are also mature, well-established companies with strong fundamentals, since entry to the DJIA requires financial stability and market relevance. This investing strategy takes advantage of the market's propensity to penalise enterprises unduly for temporary setbacks, which is based on behavioural finance anomalies such as overreaction, loss aversion, and herd behaviour.

Overreaction bias, which occurs when investors respond disproportionately to negative news or ephemeral performance difficulties, is a critical behavioural factor contributing to the Dogs of the Dow's success. When a company has difficulties—such as a poor earnings report, changes in management, or bad industry conditions—investors often project these challenges into the future, assuming they imply a long-term decline. This pessimism drives stock prices lower than fundamentals support, creating an opportunity for value-oriented strategies like the Dow Dogs. Historical data supports this theory. According to research, numerous 'dogs' have significant price recoveries over time when the market re-evaluates their underlying value.

Loss aversion, a core premise of behavioural finance, is also important. Investors are more sensitive to losses than gains, so they avoid investments considered risky or underperforming. This avoidance produces a self-perpetuating cycle in which falling prices discourage further investment, despite the company's fundamentals showing stability. The Dogs of the Dow strategy combats this aversion by deliberately focused on these underappreciated stocks, betting on their eventual restoration to average performance. During the 2008–2009 financial crisis, numerous Dow components' prices fell significantly while continuing to pay dividends. Investors that followed the Dogs of the Dow strategy during this period gained significant profits in the subsequent comeback.

The strategy takes use of herd behaviour, which is the tendency of investors to adhere to the majority. When some stocks lose popularity, they often see widespread selling as investors mimic one another's actions, regardless of their own assessments of the stock's real value. This herd-driven selling exacerbates price declines, resulting in attractive opportunities for contrarian investors. The Dogs of the Dow strategy focusses on high-yielding, undervalued stocks, using a contrarian approach to profit on price corrections when market sentiment shifts.

Empirical statistics show that the Dogs of the Dow approach has remained successful throughout time. Over the course of many decades, this technique has consistently produced competitive returns compared to the bigger market, frequently with lower volatility. Between 1973 and 2020, the method produced an average annual return of almost 14%, outperforming the DJIA's average return of nearly 11% over that time period. This outperformance is particularly impressive given the strategy's simplicity, which requires no active management or sophisticated research.

Nonetheless, the Dogs of the Dow's effectiveness comes with complexity and criticisms. One such limitation is the reliance on dividend yield as the primary selection criterion. Because declining stock prices artificially boost the yield ratio, high dividend yields may often imply financial distress. Critics argue that without a comprehensive evaluation of a company's financial soundness, investors may mistakenly choose organisations with long-term structural flaws rather than temporary challenges. In the early 2000s, high-dividend-yielding firms in the telecommunications and energy sectors underperformed due to fundamental industry shifts, emphasising the need of caution when interpreting dividend yields.

Investor behavioural biases also influence the strategy's sporadic underperformance. In bull markets, when growth businesses dominate and dividends are devalued, Dow Dogs may underperform bigger indices. This underperformance may test investors' patience and discipline, since the strategy's contrarian nature requires a willingness to reject current market trends. Many investors, swayed by short-term thinking and the allure of growth-oriented momentum, abandon the strategy during these periods, so forfeiting its long-term benefits.

Professional fund managers face tremendous job risk. Using a strategy like the Dogs of the Dow, which often involves investing in cheap firms, may result in short-term underperformance when compared to peers or benchmarks. This underperformance may discourage managers from pursuing contrarian strategies, despite their long-term potential, demonstrating the behavioural limits in the investment management business.

The Dogs of the Dow shows the enduring importance of behavioral finance. It demonstrates the persistence of market inefficiencies even inside popular indexes like the DJIA, which are known for their openness and liquidity. The strategy highlights the importance of detecting and harnessing the biases that influence investor behaviour, giving critical insights for both individual and institutional investors.

The Dogs of the Dow provides ordinary investors with a simple and practical approach to long-term investing. This strategy focusses on low-cost, dividend-paying stocks in accordance with basic value investing principles that emphasise patience, consistency, and the usefulness of compounding returns. For behavioural finance specialists, the approach provides a fascinating case study of how cognitive biases and emotional tendencies impact market dynamics, creating possibilities for those who understand and navigate these patterns.

The Dogs of the Dow is more than just an investment strategy; it represents the human side of finance. It demonstrates how psychological factors like overreaction and loss aversion contribute to market inefficiencies, as well as how disciplined, contrarian strategies may take advantage of these tendencies. In an age of algorithmic trading and data-centric analysis, the Dogs of the Dow's continued success highlights the significant impact of human psychology on markets, ensuring that behavioural finance will remain an important aspect of financial understanding for future generations.

References

Ackert, L., & Deaves, R. (2009). *Behavioral finance: Psychology, decision-making, and markets*. Cengage Learning.

Barber, B. M., & Odean, T. (2000). Trading is hazardous to your wealth: The common stock investment performance of individual investors. *The Journal of Finance, 55*(2), 773–806.

Benartzi, S., & Thaler, R. H. (1995). Myopic loss aversion and the equity. *The Quarterly Journal of Economics, 110*(1), 73–92.

Camerer, C. F., Loewenstein, G., & Prelec, D. (2004). Neuroeconomics: Why economics needs brains. *The Scandinavian Journal of Economics, 106*(3), 555–579.

De Bondt, W. F., & Thaler, R. (1985). Does the stock market overreact? *The Journal of Finance, 40*(3), 793–805.

French, K. R. (1980). Stock returns and the weekend effect. *Journal of Financial Economics, 8*(1), 55–69.

Huberman, G. (2001). Familiarity breeds investment. *The Review of Financial Studies, 14*(3), 659–680.

Jegadeesh, N., & Titman, S. (1993). Returns to buying winners and selling losers: Implications for stock market efficiency. *The Journal of Finance, 48*(1), 65–91.

Kahneman, D., & Tversky, A. (1979). Prospect theory: An analysis of decision under risk. *Econometrica, 47*(2), 263–292.

Kumar, A. (2009). Who gambles in the stock market? *The Journal of Finance, 64*(4), 1889–1933.

Laibson, D. (1997). Golden eggs and hyperbolic discounting. *The Quarterly Journal of Economics, 112*(2), 443–478.

Lakonishok, J., Shleifer, A., & Vishny, R. W. (1994). Contrarian investment, extrapolation, and risk. *The Journal of Finance, 49*(5), 1541–1578.

Liu, J., & Yu, H. H. (2024). Exploring fund management efficacy and investor behaviour in the Chinese market: An empirical insight into security selection, market timing, and cognitive biases. *International Journal of Operations and Quantitative Management, 30*(1), 112–126.

Shiller, R. J. (2000). *Irrational exuberance*. Princeton University Press.

Thaler, R., & Sunstein, C. (2008). *Nudge: Improving decisions about health, wealth, and happiness*. Penguin Books.

Part II
Behavioural Finance in Today's Markets

Transitioning from basic ideas to the dynamic reality of modern financial markets, we encounter a realm where behavioural finance has evolved from an academic curiosity into a vital framework for comprehending the disorder. In contemporary markets, marked by unparalleled speed, connection, and complexity, understanding the psychological factors influencing investor behaviour is essential. Behavioral finance in contemporary markets thoroughly examines the biases, emotional responses, and cognitive heuristics that influence the choices of millions and, collectively, the fluctuations of markets.

Contemporary financial markets are extensive ecosystems, populated by a variety of participants: experienced institutional investors, inexperienced retail traders, and algorithmic trading algorithms doing millions of transactions each second. At the core of this complex network is a singular constant—human behaviour. Notwithstanding technological advancements and data analytics, markets continue to be significantly affected by overconfidence, herd behaviour, loss aversion, and several other cognitive biases. These psychological tendencies explain why markets contradict expectations and provide a framework for traversing their erratic landscape.

This section will examine the manifestation of these biases in real-world situations, influencing market dynamics in ways that may seem unreasonable but are fundamentally human. Examine the exhilarating ascent and disastrous decline of the dot-com bubble, characterised by a widespread overvaluation of technology's capabilities that propelled stock values to unprecedented levels before the onset of reality. The 2008 financial crisis serves as a stark reminder of how overconfidence among financial institutions and a failure to acknowledge systemic dangers precipitated one of the most severe economic downturns in history. Presently, these behavioural tendencies are evident in the volatile cryptocurrency market, where fear, greed, and speculation often overshadow core principles.

These stories transcend mere historical footnotes; they serve as contemporary illustrations of behavioural finance in action. They disclose the persistent reality that markets are not exclusively regulated by numerical data, statistical analysis, or logical frameworks but rather by the emotions, prejudices, and collective psychology of the participants. This section analyses these occurrences, illuminating the cognitive pitfalls that investors encounter and the subsequent ripple effects they generate.

Consider the phenomena of meme stocks—a recent and notable illustration of how behavioural finance influences markets in the digital era. Platforms such as Reddit and Twitter have intensified herd behaviour to unparalleled extents, transforming previously obscure enterprises into market phenomena overnight. The abrupt fluctuations in companies such as GameStop and AMC are not just market oddities; they reveal how social factors, enhanced by contemporary technology, may supersede established valuation criteria and induce price swings that contradict conventional reasoning.

Likewise, the Bitcoin market, characterised by its volatile fluctuations and speculative enthusiasm, exemplifies emotional investment. In this context, fear of missing out drives purchasing frenzies, but panic selling in response to market declines underscores the influence of loss aversion. Notwithstanding the technical complexity of cryptocurrencies, the market continues to mirror human psychology—irrational, unpredictable, and profoundly affected by behavioural biases.

This portion focuses not only on comprehending the past and present but also on preparing you for the future. Through an examination of these situations, we want to demonstrate how behavioural finance provides pragmatic tools for manoeuvring through the intricacies of contemporary markets. Identifying tendencies of overconfidence may assist in circumventing the hazards of speculative bubbles. Comprehending herd behaviour allows one to withdraw as the masses surge forward. By understanding the emotional dimensions of investing, you may make judgements that are not only more astute but also more robust in the face of uncertainty.

This piece will fundamentally alter your view of financial markets. You will no longer see them as just statistics and graphs; rather, you will recognise them as dynamic systems influenced by the intricacies of human behaviour. Upon completion of this trip, you will comprehend the theoretical foundations of behavioural finance and recognise its practical significance in trend analysis, movement prediction, and risk management. In a tumultuous and uncertain financial environment, behavioural finance serves as an essential guide for those aiming to navigate with assurance and precision.

Welcome to the realm of behavioural finance in contemporary markets—a domain where psychology intersects with economics, where biases influence results, and where understanding human behaviour is essential for achieving financial success.

Chapter 4
Modern Behavioural Finance Theories

The world of finance has always been a complicated and unpredictable place, with ideas rising and falling as scientists strive to comprehend the mysterious factors that drive markets. Over the past decade, behavioural finance has seen a remarkable shift. This is no longer simply a study of biases and fundamental decision-making idiosyncrasies; it is now a cutting-edge investigation of how individuals interact with technology, social media, and algorithm-driven trading platforms in real time. In an age of rapid knowledge and digital connection, new ideas have evolved to meet contemporary investors' dynamic, technology-influenced behaviours.

These current behavioural finance theories delve further into the intricacies of human thinking, especially in response to the extraordinary speed, volume, and complexity of information. They investigate problems that standard models could never have predicted. How can human biases exhibit themselves in algorithmic trading systems? What happens when millions of investors are inundated with social media opinions in seconds? And how does our essential nature adapt to these continual changes? These new ideas reflect a reality in which finance is more than just statistics and data; it is a dynamic, adaptive system shaped by technology, human psychology, and market development (Vasileiou, 2022).

Among these recent discoveries is the adaptive market hypothesis (AMH), a ground-breaking hypothesis that claims markets change in reaction to changing circumstances, much like a living body. In this new financial ecology, survival of the fittest prevails—investors adapt, tactics alter, and the rules of the game are constantly changing. Next, the machine learning and sentiment-based asset pricing model demonstrates how algorithms can evaluate human emotion and translate it into price projections, combining technology and behavioural science to create a powerful predicting tool. We also look at the behavioural economics of algorithmic trading, which investigates how human biases may creep into seemingly 'objective' algorithms and enhance volatility. The investor overload theory investigates the influence of limitless knowledge, demonstrating that, ironically, the more investors learn, the more irrational they become (Liu et al., 2020). Finally, adaptive herding

K. L. Ooi, *Demystifying Behavioral Finance*,
https://doi.org/10.1007/978-981-96-2690-8_4

behaviour investigates how social variables alter the character of herding, changing individual investors into collective forces capable of causing market-wide transformations.

4.1 Adaptive Market Hypothesis

Consider stepping into a big, buzzing environment in which everyone is continuously evolving to survive. Some change, some fade, and some get stronger via trial and error. This is the world of finance as envisioned by Andrew Lo in his adaptive market hypothesis. AMH, which was introduced in 2004 and has gained ground in recent years, contends that markets need to be more static and consistently rational. Instead, they are dynamic, ever-changing entities in which new tactics, tools, and behaviours develop, compete, and adapt (Lo, 2004). According to Lo, the market is analogous to a natural ecosystem, and just as animals in nature must adapt to live, so must investors, enterprises, and trading techniques.

AMH is a fundamental divergence from classic ideas such as the efficient market hypothesis, which holds that markets are entirely rational and that prices always reflect all available information. AMH contends that markets are driven by their players' adaptability, particularly when they adjust to fluctuations in economic circumstances, technology, and cultural changes. Markets are continuously in motion; hence there is no one universal law regulating them under AMH. Lo proposes that when a strategy works successfully, it draws more followers—until it becomes unsuccessful, encouraging investors to change once again. This cycle of adaptation and development results in a dynamic market environment that defies the predictability of standard financial models.

Investors in AMH are not only sensible but also adaptable. They learn from previous experiences and adapt their strategy to new data, trends, and technology breakthroughs. Consider the growth of quantitative trading tactics in the early 2000s. Initially, these tactics were unique and highly lucrative, offering considerable benefits to early adopters. However, as more businesses adopted quantitative trading and algorithms got more complex, the advantage dwindled. To remain ahead, investors had to adjust again, either by refining their tactics or transitioning to new technologies such as artificial intelligence and machine learning.

What makes AMH so intriguing is its use of evolutionary ideas. Lo compares techniques to organisms in an ecosystem, with each struggling for survival. In steady market circumstances, more straightforward, time-tested tactics, such as buy-and-hold investing, may be effective. However, as market volatility increases, these tactics may be squeezed out by more aggressive, high-frequency trading approaches that thrive in fast-paced, unpredictable situations (Raimundo Júnior et al., 2022). Investors who fail to adapt risk falling behind, but those who develop thrive, reinforcing the 'survival of the fittest' dynamic in finance.

Consider a young investor called Alex, who joins the stock market at a time of great technical innovation. When Alex initially begins, standard buy-and-hold techniques are popular. Seasoned investors advise him to buy reliable, blue-chip companies and 'hold on for the long haul'. Following this guidance, Alex carefully constructs a portfolio of dependable, high-dividend firms and watches as his assets progressively increase over the following several years (Boutros et al., 2020). Life seems basic, predictable, and even easy.

But as time passes, Alex senses the landscape changing. High-frequency trading (HFT) businesses start making headlines with their lightning-fast algorithms, and tales emerge about their incredible ability to execute transactions in fractions of a second, benefitting from minute market movements. Traditional techniques need to gain ground for these new algorithm-driven solutions. Alex's buy-and-hold portfolio is not doing as well as it once did, and he feels as if he is in a whole new market (Baek & Lee, 2021). Curious, Alex chooses to adapt and begins experimenting with algorithmic trading, hoping that this new method will keep him competitive.

For a time, Alex rides the wave of high-frequency trading, enthralled by the rapid speed of his new method. However, the market continues to change. Soon, Alex realises that the HFT advantage is disappearing as more investors enter the algorithmic field, making it increasingly difficult to achieve consistent gains. Just as he starts to question his new plan, another upheaval occurs in the market: machine learning and artificial intelligence enter the picture. The industry is buzzing about predictive algorithms and sentiment analysis, which are fuelled by massive data sets and faster-than-ever processing capabilities.

Alex notices another shift and pivots once again, investing in cutting-edge AI systems to analyse market sentiment. His new technique enables him to catch patterns as they emerge, sometimes even forecasting price changes based on real-time news moods and social media trends. However, he has already learnt that markets do not remain constant. They are continually developing and adapting to new techniques that attract more followers. He knows that every advantage is just transitory.

Then, a market slump occurs. During this tumultuous moment, Alex observes that his AI models are acting strangely, forecasting patterns that do not materialise as investors flee to safety assets. It is as if the market has 'adapted' to the downturn, and surviving requires abandoning high-risk techniques. Recognising this trend, Alex returns to safer, more conservative assets, resulting in a more robust portfolio that can endure unpredictability.

The adaptive market hypothesis is powerfully demonstrated during Alex's trip. Markets, like ecosystems, are continually changing, and each new approach faces the challenges of adaptation and competition. Alex's success is dependent not on identifying a single 'perfect' technique but on his ability to recognise changes in the environment and adapt his approach appropriately. According to AMH, survival and profitability depend on flexibility, an adaptable mindset, and an understanding that what works today may not work tomorrow.

AMH also emphasises the importance of emotions and cognitive biases, claiming that these human characteristics are adaptations rather than faults. During times of severe stress, like as market crashes or economic downturns, behaviours like loss aversion and herd behaviour become more evident because they serve a protective purpose. To avoid perceived concerns, investors naturally gravitate towards safer assets or exit the market. Rather than perceiving these behaviours as illogical, AMH sees them as adaptive reactions required for survival in an unpredictable world. The theory, therefore, bridges the gap between behavioural finance and classical finance by demonstrating how biases may occasionally boost survival rates under volatile market condition.

AMH has significant ramifications for contemporary finance. It implies that there is no 'one-size-fits-all' strategy for investment since market dynamics evolve with time. Strategies that worked yesterday may become outdated tomorrow, and success goes to those who can adapt the fastest. For investors, AMH is both a warning and an invitation to innovate. It means that, rather than seeking a single ideal investing plan, investors should prioritise adaptability, learning, and the flexibility to pivot as circumstances change. This agility enables them to capitalise on changing trends and developing possibilities, seeing the market not as a problem to be solved but as an ecosystem to traverse.

4.2 Machine Learning and Sentiment-Based Asset Pricing Model

Imagine a sizeable digital universe in which every tweet, story, and headline has the power to alter markets in an instant. In this environment, when social media messages ignite transactions and news headlines affect whole industries, a new breed of investor develops. These investors, however, are not humans; instead, they are powerful machine learning algorithms that can read, analyse, and act on emotion quicker than any person. The machine learning and sentiment-based asset pricing model is a ground-breaking technique that combines the power of machine learning with behavioural finance to forecast asset values based on emotions and feelings that ripple across the digital world rather than standard measures.

At the core of this concept is the notion that sentiment—how investors perceive market circumstances and individual stocks—has a significant influence on asset values, particularly in the near term. Traditional models are based on financial accounts, economic data, and macroeconomic trends. However, sentiment, which may shift in an instant, represents a whole distinct aspect of market behaviour. A single tweet from a well-known person, a deluge of favourable reviews on a tech site, or a gloomy story may cause quick price changes that standard measurements cannot account for. The machine learning and sentiment-based asset pricing model aims to collect and quantify this fluctuating sentiment, turning words and emotions into usable data (Hirshleifer & Shumway, 2003).

To make this paradigm work, algorithms use natural language processing (NLP), a kind of artificial intelligence that reads and comprehends human language. NLP technologies analyse millions of articles, tweets, and posts to detect positive or negative sentiment towards a particular asset or the market as a whole. Consider a system that can grasp context and recognise terms like 'strong growth potential' or 'likely downturn' across large social networks and Internet platforms. These algorithms do more than count words; they recognise tone, emotion, and impact, converting raw text into sentiment ratings that reflect how the market feels about an asset at any particular time.

Consider this hypothetical scenario: word comes that a tech behemoth is introducing a ground-breaking new product. Social media surges with enthusiasm, investors and experts provide excellent evaluations, and hashtags go viral. Traditionally, investors may wait for quarterly earnings reports to determine whether this new introduction increases revenue, but a sentiment-driven algorithm recognises the opportunity much sooner. It detects a rise in positive language and quickly anticipates a short-term price jump, enabling sentiment-based traders to get ahead of the curve. This agility is critical to the model's success since it uses real-time sentiment to produce predictions that conventional analysis would have missed.

However, sentiment analysis goes beyond just determining positives or dislikes. Modern algorithms can measure sentiment intensity, determining how strongly the public feels about certain news. A modestly good review, for example, may generate a little increase, but a deluge of euphoric, high-intensity reviews might spark a purchasing frenzy. Sentiment-based models collect these subtleties and input them into machine learning algorithms, which update and recalibrate as sentiment changes. When optimism reaches a fever pitch, the system may even predict a likely correction, enabling traders to plan for both the highs and lows of sentiment-based volatility.

However, the machine learning and sentiment-based asset pricing model has complications. One problem is filtering out the noise, which is an extraneous conversation that might misrepresent actual feelings. Only some trending subjects or popular tweets are meaningful, and computers must learn to filter through the voluminous feeds, separating critical information from noise. They are taught to identify reputable sources and reject unsubstantiated rumours, ensuring that the mood index represents true market sentiment rather than transitory fads. As a consequence, these models improve over time, gaining the capacity to distinguish trustworthy signals from emotional outbursts and passing trends.

Furthermore, sentiment-based pricing is especially effective in high-volatility markets. During times of uncertainty—whether a pandemic, political upheaval, or a tech boom—traditional models often fail, as data from balance sheets and earnings reports fails to keep up with fast market changes. Sentiment-driven models shine here, using real-time data to capture the collective mood in ways that static measures cannot. As investor emotions fluctuate, the model adjusts, enabling it to flourish in situations where conventional analysis fails. It is a model based on current information flows, reflecting a market in which news travels in seconds and sentiment changes even quicker (DellaVigna & Pollet, 2009).

This methodology provides a new frontier in behavioural finance, transforming emotion from an abstract idea to a measurable asset. Machine learning is ushering in a new era of behavioural finance in which investor emotions and market forecasts coexist as part of a unified system. By including emotion in the pricing model, this method gets into the human aspect of finance—our hopes, anxieties, and reactions—and converts them into data points that determine the future of trade. The machine learning and sentiment-based asset pricing model advances behavioural finance into the digital age, where computers capture emotions and drive markets like never before.

4.3 Behavioural Economics of Algorithmic Trading

In the sleek, fast-paced world of algorithmic trading, choices are expected to be clean, flawless, and free of human mistakes. Algorithms, after all, are the ultimate rational agents, engineered to execute transactions with accuracy and speed, exploiting minute price differences and earning gains in milliseconds. They symbolise the apex of contemporary finance—mechanical, faultless, and supposedly bias-free. The behavioral economics of algorithmic trading, however, challenges this concept. According to this hypothesis, even the most advanced algorithms, which are intended to be absolutely logical, are susceptible to human interference. In reality, they may accentuate the biases that they were designed to prevent, resulting in a new species of market behaviours that combine mechanical accuracy with uniquely human irrationality (Coval & Shumway, 2005).

Consider a hedge fund using an algorithm developed to take advantage of momentum trading—the tactic of purchasing rising equities and selling falling ones. On the surface, this strategy seems rational, even ingenious. However, this algorithm incorporates data points acquired from human traders, who often include behavioural biases like as overconfidence, herd behaviour, and recency bias (the propensity to overvalue recent information). As the computer 'learns' from this data, it develops a sense of false overconfidence, making higher bets on recent trends and following the herd as it pursues rising stocks. The program is no longer simply rational; it is replicating the psychological peculiarities of the traders it was designed to surpass.

This combination of computer logic and human prejudice is not just theoretical; it occurs in actual markets every day, resulting in what some have dubbed 'artificial irrationality'. For example, at times of high volatility, computers trained on data from panic-driven transactions may begin executing sell orders quicker than human traders, worsening downward price spirals. In an instant, what was meant as a plan to capitalise on tiny, logical price swings transforms into a supercharged engine of fear-driven selling, exacerbating the exact volatility it was supposed to mitigate. These purportedly emotionless computers unwittingly replicate the market's worries, exacerbating swings and hastening market declines.

Consider this hypothetical scenario: a well-known technology business issues a significant product recall. Within seconds, news feeds and social media are flooded with debates, and algorithms throughout the market swing into high gear. One system, trained to detect negative sentiment, initiates a vast sell order in response to the unexpected influx of negative keywords. Another algorithm notices the price reduction and, using a momentum technique, starts selling as well. Soon, a cascade of algorithms will be responding to one another's moves. What would have been a slight fall if left to human traders turns into a rapid, catastrophic collapse as algorithms reinforce one other's conclusions. The behavioural echo chamber formed by these algorithms magnifies a single statement into a financial tsunami.

This theory emphasises the role of confirmation bias in algorithmic trading. When programmers create trading algorithms, they often base them on patterns that they hope will regularly generate profits. However, they may unwittingly inject confirmation bias into the system, teaching it to recognise signals that support previous notions. For example, an algorithm intended to favour technology stocks may be more likely to interpret data signals positively, reinforcing an optimistic outlook even when the facts do not support it. As a consequence, the algorithm acts like an overconfident trader, doubling back on sectors it 'believes' will increase, potentially leading to catastrophic mispricing when the bubble collapses.

Another noteworthy aspect of the behavioral economics of algorithmic trading is the phenomena of herding behaviour—but in this situation, algorithms follow other algorithms. In classical finance, herd behaviour refers to how investors often replicate the behaviours of others, resulting in feedback loops that inflate asset values during bubbles and intensify declines during crashes. With algorithms, this impact may occur quickly, with each algorithm responding not just to price fluctuations but also to the trading patterns of other algorithms. In seconds, a minor price rise may activate purchase orders across dozens of algorithms, resulting in a fast price increase with little underlying value change.

These actions have far-reaching consequences. In human-dominated marketplaces, herd behaviour may occur across days or weeks, allowing for contemplation, reconsideration, and correction. However, when algorithms herd, the timeframe shrinks to just seconds. This fast escalation may cause prices to reach extreme highs or lows almost rapidly, resulting in flash crashes—sudden, abrupt falls in asset values that often rebound swiftly but leave havoc in their wake (Statman, 2014). These collapses underscore the unexpected effects of algorithmic herding, in which robots' purported neutrality reflects—and usually magnifies—the aggregate irrationality of human traders.

For investors and financial institutions, the behavioural economics of algorithmic trading is a two-edged sword. On the one hand, algorithms provide remarkable efficiency and can handle massive volumes of data in ways that human brains cannot. They can identify trends, adjust to market circumstances, and execute trades precisely. On the other hand, these algorithms are based on data impacted by human psychology, and they operate in markets that are naturally emotional and turbulent. Their acts, although quick and deliberate, might introduce new biases into the market, resulting in self-perpetuating cycles of irrationality.

4.4 Investor Overload Theory

Traders in the golden era of Wall Street lived by a single mantra: knowledge is power. And, in today's digital environment, investors have never had greater access to knowledge—or what seems to be. Every second, their screens are bombarded with breaking news headlines, real-time stock tickers, earnings call transcripts, tweets from financial influencers, and an unending stream of notifications. It is a long cry from the days when investors checked the morning paper for information or watched an evening program for a review. However, as investors are realising, having a wealth of knowledge does not always lead to sound judgements. Enter the investor overload theory, which contends that this continual flood of information is less a tool for success and more a prescription for worry and rash decisions.

Consider Emma, a young professional who just began investing. She is ambitious, well informed, and diligent in her studies. Every morning, she examines market summaries, industry news, and analyst opinions. However, her phone rapidly fills up with alerts about interest rate changes, social media talk about her favourite equities, and a push alert about a company's quarterly earnings release. Emma's meticulously curated research turns into a tidal wave, and the strain to absorb every bit of knowledge starts to take its toll. By lunchtime, she is overwhelmed, unable to distinguish good ideas from the cacophony. Instead of making educated judgements, she is left feeling paralysed.

Investor overload theory investigates the consequences of this constant data influx on our cognitive abilities. Behavioural economists such as Michael Barber and Terrance Odean contend that when investors are presented with too much information, their ability to absorb it rationally deteriorates—overwhelmed by constant inputs, the brain resorts to mental shortcuts—quick, intuitive judgements designed to simplify the job at hand. This is where the recency bias comes in. Because Emma has so much to go through, she begins to concentrate on the most recent, emotionally intense updates. A flood of bad news about an industry downturn might cause her to sell in a panic, even if her long-term investing plan remains intact.

However, the impact of information overload extends deeper, resulting in an even more insidious prejudice: confirmation bias. When presented with several sources, investors tend to lean towards those that reinforce their existing beliefs. Emma, who is optimistic about technology, may ignore warnings of a probable slump in the industry, preferring to focus on any positive expectations. In this overloaded condition, she takes solace in supporting her ideas, even if it means disregarding warning flags. This selective information processing maintains her in an echo chamber, reinforcing her original attitude while concealing potential threats.

Information overload also causes what psychologists refer to as decision fatigue. Emma devotes so much time and energy to sorting through material that by the time she reaches a choice, her mental energy is depleted. This exhaustion causes one of two outcomes: she either delays making a choice or defaults to what the crowd is doing. And here is when things become dicey. When investors get overloaded, they tend to follow the crowd's lead—buying when others buy and selling when others sell—regardless of whether it corresponds with their plan. Herd behaviour, fuelled by tiredness, exacerbates market volatility, pushing prices up unreasonably or causing abrupt drops due to rumours and superficial trends.

The consequence of investor overload goes well beyond individual holdings. As more investors succumb to the continual data stream, markets become more sensitive to passing news events and less grounded in fundamentals. In this loud environment, even the slightest hint of a recession, inflation, or geopolitical conflict may set off a wave of panic selling or euphoric purchasing. Consider an earnings report with a little revenue shortfall—investors, overwhelmed by a flood of alerts, overreact, leading the stock price to plummet. When a tiny piece of information is exaggerated by investor saturation, it becomes a market-moving event.

Ironically, the investor overload theory demonstrates that in finance, more knowledge does not imply more excellent performance. Instead, investors become more prone to emotion-driven decision-making, relying on surface-level patterns rather than in-depth study. As a consequence, the idea calls into question the notion that being connected at all times is good. To deal with information overload, investors are increasingly turning to technologies that help filter, organise, and distil data. Platforms that deliver just the most critical updates or summarise news trends are becoming more popular, providing investors with a break from the never-ending digital flow.

But the ultimate conclusion from investor overload theory might be a lesson in self-control. Just as athletes exercise their bodies, investors may need to train their brains, focusing on filtering out irrelevant information and adhering to their plans. Setting limits, such as planned check-ins rather than continual updates, allows investors to retake control and concentrate on what is really important. In a society preoccupied with connectedness, the ability to filter may be the contemporary investor's most valuable attribute.

4.5 Adaptive Herding Behaviour

If you have ever looked through social media and had an uncontrollable want to join a group, you have felt the lure of herding behaviour. However, in the realm of finance, this natural tendency to follow the crowd has evolved into something considerably more powerful. Adaptive herding behaviour is a phenomenon peculiar to our hyperconnected society, in which individual actions are changed by fast input from millions of others. It is digital herding, fuelled by algorithms, social networks, and an unwavering determination to stay caught up.

Consider John, a casual investor, who gets onto his social media account one morning to discover his timeline is buzzing about a new biotech company. The early enthusiasm seems to be restrained, with just a few postings from financial influencers he follows. However, within hours, the tale took on a life of its own, fuelled by retweets, shares, and comments. Friends, influencers, and even strangers from his online investing group are buying in, hailing the stock as a 'must-have'. John, who had never heard of the firm before, is suddenly filled with both enthusiasm and a sense of urgency. The more he sees others getting involved, the more he thinks he will lose his opportunity. So he buys in—not because he has done any study on the firm but because everyone else appears to believe it is a great opportunity.

Adaptive herding behaviour varies from conventional herding in that the fast-paced, linked nature of digital platforms drives it. In earlier decades, investors may have taken the counsel of a broker or analyst. Today, views spread at the pace of retweets, with each sharing magnifying the original feeling. A single tweet from a prominent influencer may transform a tiny stock into a hot issue, triggering a chain reaction that entices even the most sceptical investors. In today's digital era, herding is more than simply following; it is about responding in real time to the swarm of voices booming over social media and forums.

The fear of missing out, or FOMO, is essential to adaptive herding. Every investor has seen others earn rapid riches, and the fear of missing out motivates them to act without adequately analysing the circumstances. Each notice and update heightens John's FOMO, and each post makes him feel like the clock is ticking (Liu et al., 2020). This sense of urgency drives him to purchase without hesitation, not out of solid reasoning but out of dread of regret. Social media sites, mindful of FOMO's power, use algorithms to elevate popular material, which means that as more people debate a stock, it gets more prominent, attracting new investors.

WallStreetBets, a Reddit community, has elevated adaptive herding to a communal phenomenon. In early 2021, WallStreetBets staged a massive short squeeze on GameStop, bringing together thousands of individual investors in a concerted campaign against institutional short sellers. This was not classic herding; instead, it was a type of digital tribalism in which members exchanged thoughts, supported one another, and reinforced their collective determination. The outcome was a price increase that defied all market fundamentals, as individual buyers converted the stock into a symbol of resistance to Wall Street. Adaptive herding, in this case, was more than simply following the crowd; it was about joining a movement motivated by a common goal and aided by the reach of internet forums.

The scope of adaptive herding is expanded by algorithms meant to promote hot topics. When a stock or asset attracts attention, social media algorithms promote it to additional people, resulting in a feedback cycle in which exposure generates interest, which in turn raises visibility. John's first exposure to the biotech stock was no accident—it was intentionally placed by an algorithm that recognised its rising popularity. With each like, share, and retweet, the algorithm increases the stock's visibility, which fuels the loop. Adaptive herding becomes a nearly self-sustaining process in which human psychology and machine learning combine to form a market force that is difficult to resist.

In the financial sector, this occurrence has far-reaching implications. When adaptive herding takes hold, asset values might rise or fall according to collective feelings rather than economic realities. John's choice to acquire biotech stock, which is shared by thousands of others, propels the price to false highs. However, when the mood cools, the plunge is just as quick, trapping investors like John in a downward spiral. Adaptive herding produces bubbles that may rupture without notice just as soon as they develop. It is a force that feeds on velocity but seldom maintains it, leaving a path of uncertainty and, for many, regret.

The lesson of adaptive herding behaviour is a warning one. In today's hyperconnected society, choices are often made with others. Investors are part of a more extensive ecosystem in which each activity affects and is impacted by others. Understanding adaptive herding requires contemporary investors to recognise when a choice is motivated by actual thinking and when it is merely an instinctual reaction to the mob. It serves as a reminder that, although trends are appealing, they are often fleeting, based on perception rather than truth (Loang, 2025).

Adaptive herding demonstrates the fundamentally social character of today's markets. It is a phenomenon that transforms individual deals into collective movements, with the might of the public pushing prices to dizzying heights and unexpected lows. To navigate this world, investors like John must be sceptical, patient, and prepared to ignore the crowd's seductive appeal. The one certainty in adaptive herding is that the mob will disperse as fast as it forms, leaving those who followed its call trying to make sense of what remains.

References

Baek, S., & Lee, K. Y. (2021). The risk transmission of COVID-19 in the US stock market. *Applied Economics, 53*(17), 1976–1990.

Boutros, M., Ben-David, I., Graham, J. R., Harvey, C. R., & Payne, J. W. (2020). *The persistence of miscalibration*. National Bureau of Economic Research.

Coval, J. D., & Shumway, T. (2005). Do behavioral biases affect prices? *The Journal of Finance, 60*(1), 1–34.

DellaVigna, S., & Pollet, J. M. (2009). Investor inattention and Friday earnings announcements. *The Journal of Finance, 64*(2), 709–749.

Hirshleifer, D., & Shumway, T. (2003). Good day sunshine: Stock returns and the weather. *The Journal of Finance, 58*(3), 1009–1032.

Liu, Y., Sun, Q., & Wu, L. (2020). Sentiment-based investment strategies: A machine learning perspective. *Journal of Behavioral Finance, 21*(4), 341–359.

Lo, A. W. (2004). Adaptive markets: A financial evolutionary theory. *Journal of Portfolio Management, 30*(5), 15–29.

Loang, O. K. (2025). Can machine learning surpass human investors? Evidence from adaptive herding behaviour in US, China and India. *Journal of Applied Economics, 28*(1), 2435796.

Raimundo Júnior, G. D. S., Palazzi, R. B., Tavares, R. D. S., & Klotzle, M. C. (2022). Market stress and herding: A new approach to the cryptocurrency market. *Journal of Behavioral Finance, 23*(1), 43–57.

Statman, M. (2014). Behavioral finance: Finance with normal people. *Borsa Istanbul Review, 14*(2), 65–73.

Vasileiou, E. (2022). Behavioral finance and market efficiency in the time of the COVID-19 pandemic: does fear drive the market?. In *The Political Economy of Covid-19* (pp. 116–133). Routledge.

Chapter 5
Practical Applications and Case Studies

This chapter begins with a promise: to reveal how behavioural finance theories come to life in actual markets, where investor psychology influences price movements, trends, and the boom-and-bust cycles that characterise economic history. Every market movement in finance tells a tale about ambition, anxiety, greed, and, on rare occasions, extreme danger. This chapter delves into such experiences, demonstrating how ideas like overconfidence, herding, emotion, and speculation manifest themselves not just in academic models but also in the fundamental choices of millions of investors over time. We experience the real-world influence of psychological biases and social dynamics via crucial market events when a single, apparently minor action may cascade into a phenomenon that captures—and captivates—entire populations.

We will look at how psychology influences not just individual transactions but also the larger patterns that push prices to illogical highs and unsustainable lows. In these case studies, notions of FOMO, loss aversion, and overreaction are tested in high-stakes marketplaces, altering businesses and, in some cases, whole economies. As we go through these historical and contemporary market occurrences, we will discover truths that transcend any one market or asset, providing timeless lessons on the persistent power of human psychology in finance. These tales are as much about people as they are about money, illustrating the emotions and hazards that transform markets into places of success and caution.

5.1 Apple's Brand Loyalty and Investor Overconfidence

Apple is more than simply a technology corporation; it is a worldwide phenomenon with a cult-like following. For investors, Apple's brand devotion has resulted in one of the most reliable stock investments in modern financial history. Owning Apple shares has become a source of pride, a sign of belonging to a firm that has changed

K. L. Ooi, *Demystifying Behavioral Finance*,
https://doi.org/10.1007/978-981-96-2690-8_5

industries and revolutionised personal technology. This significant connection to Apple's brand and stock price may be explained by behavioural finance concepts such as the endowment effect and overconfidence bias, which cause investors to cling to their shares while ignoring possible hazards in favour of unshakeable confidence in Apple's future.

Since going public, Apple's stock has risen by a phenomenal 107,000% (as of 2021), resulting in innumerable wealthy investors and cementing Apple's position as a foundation of global portfolios. For Apple shareholders, this success has generated a profound endowment effect—an emotional connection that makes it difficult to sell shares, even when facts sometimes indicate caution. According to behavioural finance studies, investors place a higher value on assets they currently possess than they would otherwise. Apple's 'endowment effect' is heightened by its brand's emotional resonance; choosing to keep Apple shares seems not just financially sensible but also emotionally fulfilling.

Overconfidence bias is a critical factor in Apple's market domination. Investors often think that Apple's track record of success ensures a future of consistent growth despite the fact that the IT sector is characterised by fast upheaval and intense competition. The notion that 'Apple will always be Apple' feeds overconfidence, causing investors to ignore indicators of market saturation or economic challenges that might affect profitability. According to behavioural finance, overconfidence may bias decision-making, causing investors to underestimate risks. Apple's fantastic track record of innovation—iPhones, Apple Watch, AirPods—feeds into this bias, making it easy to think that the company will stay unrivalled.

Furthermore, Apple's power goes beyond its stock. It is a crucial position in almost every primary index and exchange traded funds (ETFs), so investors who do not directly own Apple are nonetheless exposed to its performance. This broad ownership creates a herding effect in which investors rely on Apple as a dependable, 'must-have' item in their portfolios. Apple's stock split and the unveiling of new 5G iPhones increased the company's worth to more than $2 trillion in 2020 alone, demonstrating the collective belief in its long-term potential. However, behavioural finance teaches us that such dependence may lead to market weaknesses if mood shifts—a potent warning that even apparently impenetrable equities are vulnerable to the market's emotional currents.

Apple's success story demonstrates the attractiveness of brand loyalty, the strength of overconfidence, and the endowment effect in behavioural finance. Long-term Apple investors see holding shares as more than a financial choice; it is a commitment to a vision and confidence in the power of inventio. However, as behavioural finance demonstrates, attachment and overconfidence may impair judgement, so investors must stay watchful even with the world's most beloved companies.

5.2 Nudge Theory in Retirement Savings Plans

The notion of 'nudging' in retirement savings is a masterclass in behavioural finance, where little changes in the decision-making environment lead to significant financial effects. For years, governments and businesses have struggled with the difficulty of encouraging workers to save more for retirement. Traditional efforts, such as providing information or encouraging voluntary enrolment in retirement programmes, have needed more effectiveness. Enter nudge theory, which uses status quo bias and loss aversion to boost participation rates and ensure workers' financial prospects.

Automatic enrolment in retirement plans, which is increasingly popular in many firms, is an excellent illustration of the nudge theory in action. Rather than requiring workers to sign up voluntarily, firms automatically enrol them in 401(k) plans, with the option to opt out if desired. This simple move takes advantage of status quo bias, which is the natural propensity to continue with the status quo rather than change. Most workers who are automatically enrolled stay in the plan since opting out costs effort. According to Vanguard research, automatic enrolment in retirement plans has increased participation rates from 55 to 92%, significantly boosting savings among young and low-income workers who would otherwise not join.

Loss aversion enhances the efficacy of automatic enrolment. Behavioural finance research indicates that individuals are more driven to prevent losses than to make profits. Once registered, workers are less inclined to cancel payments because they believe that opting out will result in a 'loss' of future rewards. This fear of loss motivates sustained involvement, allowing workers to increase their retirement assets without needing continual effort. Furthermore, the contribution rate is often set at a low level, which automatically increases each year, encouraging workers to save gradually. This design seems less demanding and lowers the psychological 'pain' of saving (Baek & Lee, 2021).

The success of nudging has had a significant influence not just on individual workers but also on society. Higher saving rates minimise the possibility that people would depend substantially on social services after retirement, resulting in a more financially secure society. The application of the nudge theory to retirement savings demonstrates how tiny policy adjustments guided by behavioural insights may result in significant improvements in financial behaviour. Behavioural finance continues to prove that how options are presented may be the difference between economic instability and secure retirement.

5.3 IPO Hype and Initial Price Volatility

Initial public offerings (IPOs) are sometimes shrouded in the glamour and appeal of the 'next big thing'. To investors, IPOs offer the opportunity to get in on a promising firm on the ground floor, with the prospect of enormous profits. However, this enthusiasm often results in extreme price volatility, which is driven by overconfidence, herd behaviour, and the availability heuristic. Investors rush in, fuelled by a mix of optimism and selective memory, resulting in huge demand that may drive prices skyrocketing only to fall.

IPO data demonstrates this volatility. According to Renaissance Capital, the average IPO rose 16% on its first day in 2020. However, just 28% of these companies beat the S&P 500 in the year after their IPO, demonstrating the gap between early enthusiasm and long-term success. Take Uber's 2019 IPO, for example. The business started with a value of roughly $82 billion, but its shares plunged 40% in 6 months when the market adjusted expectations to reflect actual reality. This trend exemplifies the availability heuristic in action: investors recall high-profile successes like Google or Facebook and expect that every IPO will follow the same path despite the high failure rate.

Overconfidence bias also has a significant impact. Many IPO investors feel they can pick winners based on scant information, assuming they grasp the company's prospects. This overconfidence often results in considerable demand on the first day, causing a price increase that is seldom maintained. When the initial euphoria fades, and financial facts become clear, reality frequently takes over, resulting in a sell-off as investors modify their expectations. Airbnb's IPO in December 2020 started at $146, more than double its initial price, but the shares fluctuated as concerns developed about the sustainability of its value.

Herd behaviour exacerbates IPO volatility. Investors are affected by media coverage, social media chatter, and other investors' behaviour, all of which contribute to a frenzy around IPOs. Individuals invest because they are afraid of missing out on a rich chance. After all, 'everyone else is buying'. However, as behavioural finance has shown, following the herd may be harmful in highly speculative settings. IPOs teach an essential lesson: although the enthusiasm may be contagious, investors sometimes pay a premium for hype, only to be disappointed when the price corrects. The volatility around IPOs serves as a reminder of how fast investor mood can alter, with behavioural biases fuelling early euphoria before giving way to dismal financial realities.

5.4 Black Friday and Double 11

Black Friday in the United States and Double 11 (Singles' Day) in China are two of the world's biggest shopping days, with shoppers spending billions of dollars in only a few hours. These events do more than provide discounts; they also use fear of missing out (FOMO), loss aversion, and anchoring to generate a shopping frenzy that is both psychological and financial. These discounts, according to clever marketing, have transformed shopping into a high-stakes event in which every customer feels compelled to act quickly or risk losing out (Baek & Lee, 2021).

The statistics are astonishing. Alibaba's Double 11 event earned a record-breaking $84.5 billion in sales in 2021, while Black Friday brought in $9 billion in the United States. During Double 11, sales reach hundreds of transactions per second, showing the enormous demand caused by time-sensitive agreements. These events use FOMO by giving 'flash deals' and 'lightning discounts' that expire in minutes, creating a situation in which customers feel pressured to purchase right away. According to behavioural finance, FOMO is a potent incentive, encouraging individuals to make rash choices in fear of missing out on a unique chance.

Loss aversion also plays a significant influence. Consumers are more driven to fear missing out on a bargain than to benefit from it, which businesses take advantage of by presenting discounts as limited-time specials that will not be repeated. For example, on Singles' Day, retailers display original pricing with huge discounts, emphasising the notion that declining to purchase now would result in a financial 'loss'. This framing encourages customers to spend more than they expected in order to avoid the regret of losing out on imagined savings. According to research, loss aversion may improve purchase probability by up to 30% in high-stakes sales scenarios.

Anchoring is another strategy in which sellers prominently show original pricing alongside discount prices. By anchoring the discount to a higher price, shops make the discount seem larger, enhancing the perceived value of the offer. On Black Friday, for example, a $300 TV marked down to $150 seems like a fantastic deal because the consumer's perspective is rooted in the higher price, even if the sale price is accessible all year long. This psychological deception is quite successful; research indicates that anchoring may cause customers to spend up to 50% more than they would otherwise.

5.5 Tesla's Stock Price Volatility

Few stocks captivate the public's imagination like Tesla. It is a firm that, like its mysterious CEO Elon Musk, defies convention, eliciting both ardent devotion and deep scepticism. Tesla's stock has become a phenomenon in and of itself, a battlefield for public emotion, technical ambition, and financial speculation. Its price fluctuations are a clear demonstration of sentiment-based asset pricing, overconfidence bias, and attention theory in action. Tesla's stock is impacted not just by financial reports or production statistics but also by Musk's tweets, media hype, and an almost cult-like following of retail investors who believe in Tesla's ambition to change the car industry and lead the charge towards a sustainable future.

Tesla's volatility is partly due to emotion rather than fundamentals. Every tweet from Musk, whether unveiling a new product or jokingly hinting at future intentions, has the potential to send Tesla's stock skyrocketing or plummeting. Investors have gotten used to Musk's every move, taking his statements as predictions about Tesla's future. This is not just about the company's financial success; it is about a common notion that Tesla is not your typical automobile manufacturer. Musk's personal charm and broad vision generate an aura around Tesla, causing investors to get emotionally involved in the company. Sentiment-based asset pricing is on the whole show here since the price represents not just the company's current worth but also its shareholders' collective hopes and aspirations.

This sentiment-driven approach to Tesla stock is exacerbated by overconfidence bias. Many Tesla investors, sure of the company's future domination, need to be more confident in their investment and often overlook hazards or problems. Even in the face of manufacturing delays, quality control concerns, and tough competition, Tesla's ardent believers remain steadfast, confident that the business is on track to revolutionise not just automobiles but energy, technology, and beyond. This overconfidence may verge on invincibility, with investors dismissing any unfavourable news as momentary setbacks in a long-term success narrative. For Tesla shareholders, purchasing shares is more than simply a financial choice; it is a gamble on a brighter future, a leap of faith in the power of invention and vision.

Attention theory contributes to Tesla's price volatility. In an era where stocks may rise or fall based solely on media coverage, Tesla's outsized presence in the news attracts attention. Every Tesla development is covered by news networks, financial experts, and social media platforms, with tiny changes being amplified into significant events. When Tesla announces new features, debuts a product, or achieves a milestone, the stock surges as investors hurry to respond to the latest news. This ongoing focus produces a feedback loop in which high exposure generates curiosity, which in turn drives price movement. Tesla's stock becomes a tale, and everyone—investors, analysts, admirers, and sceptics—wishes to be a part of it.

Tesla's attention-driven volatility was arguably best shown in 2020 when the company's stock surged more than 700% amid uncertain fundamentals. The price was influenced by a combination of excitement about electric cars, Musk's visibility, and the widespread assumption that Tesla was on track to become the market leader. Retail investors flocked to platforms like Robinhood, fuelled by promises of enormous profits and the attraction of owning a piece of the future. But, as with all sentiment-driven moves, volatility is unavoidable. Any whiff of bad news—a regulatory crackdown, a competitor's breakthrough, or manufacturing setbacks—can lead the stock to collapse just as rapidly, leaving overconfident investors confronted with hazards they previously disregard.

The influence of emotion and overconfidence on Tesla's stock has created a 'love it or hate it' division among investors. While some regard Tesla as a game changer, others see it as a bubble about to burst. This polarisation generates a peculiar tension, with each side hoping to be proved correct. Short sellers and sceptics have gambled against Tesla's stock, claiming that its lofty value is unsustainable and unsupported by conventional criteria. True believers, however, remain undaunted, confident that Tesla is more than a vehicle business; it is a movement. This division exacerbates the stock's volatility, as each new piece of news either boosts the belief of its supporters or emboldens its detractors.

Tesla's narrative demonstrates how public mood, overconfidence, and media attention may combine to produce a volatile, high-risk stock. It is more than simply the company's sales or profit margins; it is also about what Tesla symbolises to its shareholders. For many, Tesla represents a future they want to believe in, and they are ready to ignore short-term problems in order to be a part of that vision (Liu et al., 2020). However, for every increase, there is a decrease, and for every investor who views Tesla as the future, there is another who says it is overrated. The conflict between confidence and scepticism propels Tesla's stock to heights and depths that other firms seldom witness, reminding us that in the world of high-profile equities, mood can be just as potent as profits.

Finally, Tesla's stock volatility reflects contemporary finance, where the distinction between fact and perception is often blurred. It serves as a reminder that in markets, conviction is firm, and when paired with attentiveness and overconfidence, it may result in movements that defy conventional reasoning. For Tesla supporters, the stock is more than simply an investment; it demonstrates their faith in the power of innovation (Vasileiou, 2022). And as long as Tesla's tale captivates the public, its stock will reflect the enthusiasm, confidence, and unpredictable nature of people who believe in it.

As we peel back the layers of these market events, we can see how human psychology influences both the rise and fall of speculative bubbles. Overconfidence and herd mentality, as well as the unquenchable dread of losing out, demonstrate how feeling and belief may create the appearance of everlasting riches. This chapter presents a clear picture of the enthralling but hazardous dance between hope and reality, demonstrating that, although the assets vary, the appeal of rapid money and the emotional forces behind it remain ageless. The tales herein are a compelling reminder of the narrow line between profit and loss, encapsulating the adrenaline and agony that have marked financial speculation throughout history.

References

Ackert, L. F., & Deaves, R. (2009). *Behavioral finance: Psychology, decision-making, and markets*. South-Western Cengage Learning.

Baek, S., & Lee, K. Y. (2021). The risk transmission of COVID-19 in the US stock market. *Applied Economics, 53*(17), 1976–1990.

Barberis, N., & Thaler, R. (2003). A survey of behavioral finance. In G. M. Constantinides, M. Harris, & R. M. Stulz (Eds.), *Handbook of the economics of finance* (Vol. 1, pp. 1053–1128). Elsevier.

Boutros, M., Ben-David, I., Graham, J. R., Harvey, C. R., & Payne, J. W. (2020). *The persistence of miscalibration*. National Bureau of Economic Research.

Glaser, M., & Weber, M. (2007). Overconfidence and trading volume. *The Geneva Risk and Insurance Review, 32*, 1–36.

Kahneman, D. (2011). *Thinking, fast and slow*. Farrar, Straus, and Giroux.

Liu, Y., Sun, Q., & Wu, L. (2020). Sentiment-based investment strategies: A machine learning perspective. *Journal of Behavioral Finance, 21*(4), 341–359.

Lo, A. W. (2004). Adaptive markets: A financial evolutionary theory. *Journal of Portfolio Management, 30*(5), 15–29.

Loang, K. O. (2024). Adaptive herding in the age of algorithms: Behavioral insights from WallStreetBets. *Behavioral Finance Journal, 33*(2), 112–134.

Odean, T. (1998). Are investors reluctant to realize their losses? *The Journal of Finance, 53*(5), 1775–1798.

Shiller, R. J. (2000). *Irrational exuberance*. Princeton University Press.

Statman, M. (2017). *Finance for normal people: How investors and markets behave*. Oxford University Press.

Thaler, R. H., & Sunstein, C. R. (2008). *Nudge: Improving decisions about health, wealth, and happiness*. Penguin Books.

Vasileiou, E. (2022). Behavioral finance and market efficiency in the time of the COVID-19 pandemic: Does fear drive the market? In *The political economy of COVID-19* (pp. 116–133). Routledge.

Chapter 6
Behavioural Finance and Financial Crises

Financial crises do not arise by chance; they are the result of market psychology, fuelled by human emotion and propelled by the unrelenting pull of greed, fear, and the constant hope that 'this time is different'. This chapter delves into the underlying psychological processes that underlay some of history's most iconic financial catastrophes, from centuries-old bubbles and manias to modern-day gut-wrenching disasters. Behind every speculative frenzy, every unexpected market crash, and every frantic bailout is a labyrinth of cognitive biases, collective behaviours, and irrational judgements that transform financial institutions into ticking time bombs.

This is a voyage into the darker side of market psychology, where overconfidence blinds investors to danger, herd behaviour propels prices to absurd heights, and panic selling throws whole economies into a downward spiral. As we investigate these crises, we will discover that behavioural finance principles are more than just ideas; they are concrete forces that may shape—or shatter—fortunes, policies, and lives. The purpose of this chapter is to illustrate the human factor underlying market breakdowns, demonstrating that financial crises are as much a narrative of psychology as they are about economics.

6.1 The Tulip Mania: A Lesson in Speculative Frenzy

In the early 1600s, the Dutch Republic was more than simply a centre of commerce and luxury; it was the throbbing heart of Europe's Golden Age, teeming with Eastern treasures. Among the exotic items filling Dutch marketplaces was a brilliant new flower: the tulip. The tulip, imported from the Ottoman Empire, was unlike anything the Dutch had seen before. Its vibrant colours, unusual variances, and distinctive patterns made it a premium commodity sought by the wealthy elite (Raimundo Júnior et al., 2022). Tulips became a status symbol, representing one's riches and

K. L. Ooi, *Demystifying Behavioral Finance*,
https://doi.org/10.1007/978-981-96-2690-8_6

social standing. So, a tiny flower sparked one of history's most famous financial bubbles: Tulip Mania.

Tulips were formerly considered a luxury item for aristocracy and botanists who valued their unusual appearance. However, the attractiveness of the flower was contagious. Tulip prices rose as demand increased, converting the flower from a symbol of wealth to a speculative asset. Some tulips grew flame-like, multi-coloured petals as a result of a virus that produced unusual patterns, increasing their value. Tulip prices surged, and they moved from garden variety to cultural phenomenon. By the early 1630s, buying a rare tulip was equivalent to owning a work of art, a symbol of one's riches and taste, and, more crucially, a ticket to future prosperity.

The craze quickly spread to the broader population, and everyone from farmers to fishermen wanted in on the fun. A single tulip bulb might garner prices that appear absurd even by today's standards. At the peak of the fever in 1636, a single Semper Augustus bulb was reputedly sold for 6000 florins—the price of a home on Amsterdam's most extensive canal. To put this into context, 6000 florins was nearly ten times the yearly salary of a competent worker. However, in a frantic market, these prices seemed acceptable. Prices continued to rise as long as consumers expected them to. Tulips became a speculative ticket to quick riches, with everyone believing they might find a 'greater fool' prepared to pay even more.

The tulip market became self-sustaining due to speculation. Buyers and sellers traded on credit, paying with promissory notes rather than cash. This permitted people to purchase tulips they could not afford in the expectation of selling them for a profit. Taverns transformed into makeshift markets where 'tulip futures' were traded without anybody ever seeing the bulbs. Tulip business thrived on trust, with purchasers pledging to pay later and believing that prices would only grow. By winter 1636, bulbs had yet to bud and were being sold only on conjecture (Glaser & Weber, 2007). People bought and traded promises rather than flowers, with each transaction increasing prices and reinforcing the impression that tulips were worth every cent.

However, the tulip market, like all bubbles, was founded on thin air and could not exist indefinitely. By February 1637, rumours of a decline had circulated across the market. A few sellers attempted to pay out, and panic set in. As prices started to fall, the communal optimism that had previously propelled prices upward shattered. Tulips that were once worth a fortune turned almost worthless in a matter of days. A bulb that had formerly cost hundreds of florins was now just worth a common vegetable. The bubble burst, and when investors saw their assets were worthless, a wave of financial devastation spread throughout the Dutch economy.

The aftermath was catastrophic. Fortunes vanished, obligations remained unfulfilled, and debtors faced catastrophe. Thousands of Dutch individuals were left impoverished after investing their money, houses, and futures in tulips. Lawsuits for unfulfilled contracts inundated the courts as creditors attempted to recoup their losses. The Dutch government contemplated intervening to stabilise the market but eventually decided not to, allowing the nation to deal with the consequences on its own. Tulip Mania left a lasting impression on the Dutch mentality, serving as a cautionary tale against speculative extravagance.

Tulip Mania serves as a cautionary story on crowd behaviour and overconfidence bias. The enthusiasm was not motivated by a reasonable appraisal of worth; instead, it was fuelled by a widespread notion that tulips might lead to riches. People rushed in not because of the bulbs' inherent value but because others were purchasing. The end consequence was a self-reinforcing cycle in which higher prices justified further speculation. Overconfidence was a significant factor, as many disregarded warnings and staked their fortunes on a market that defied logic. The assumption that tulip prices will only rise blinded investors to the hazards.

Fear of missing out (FOMO) was an additional potent influence. Watching others get rich via tulips was too enticing to pass up. Even others who were initially wary joined the fever, concerned that if they did not act, they would be left behind (Boutros et al., 2020). This societal pressure, along with the promise of easy money, warped logical judgement and inflated the bubble to unsustainable levels. The temptation of tulip money turned reasonable people into speculators, following a delusion that would ultimately lead to financial devastation.

Centuries later, Tulip Mania's lessons remain relevant. Like the dot-com bubble and current cryptocurrency booms, it reminds us that in finance, human emotion sometimes trumps logic. The excitement of speculation, the promise of rapid fortune, and the conviction that 'this time is different' continue to drive markets today. Tulip Mania remains a vivid reminder of the dangers inherent in speculative frenzy—a tale of beauty, ambition, and the fatal seduction of quick money.

6.2 1997 Asian Financial Crisis: The Collapse of the "Asian Miracle"

In the early 1990s, Southeast Asia's thriving economy was the envy of the globe. Thailand, Indonesia, South Korea, and Malaysia, known as the 'Asian Tigers', were enjoying double-digit growth rates, with rising GDPs and swelling middle classes. Foreign investors were fascinated by the so-called Asian Miracle, assuming that these countries had unlocked the recipe for endless prosperity. Behind the scenes, however, fractures were starting to appear, concealed by a heady combination of overconfidence, herd behaviour, and rampant speculation. In 1997, the mirage of limitless progress collapsed almost instantly, sparking a crisis that would wipe away billions of dollars in wealth, destabilise governments, and leave a permanent mark on the region's economy.

The Asian Financial Crisis is often used as a case study in overconfidence bias. Local and foreign investors poured money into Southeast Asian markets, believing that the region's prosperity was certain. Banks throughout Asia made aggressive loans, fuelled by the expectation that property prices and stock markets would continue to increase. The real estate industry thrived, with developments funded by billions of dollars in loans, much of which were short-term, foreign-denominated debt. In Thailand, for example, foreign debt as a proportion of GDP had risen to

50% by 1996, with private sector debt reaching 1.6 times the country's GDP. Despite these warning indicators, the general feeling was one of unwavering optimism. The Asian Tigers appeared invincible.

By 1996, Thailand's economy was showing symptoms of distress. Real estate values, which had been rising at unsustainable rates, began to decline, leaving banks and investors vulnerable. The Thai baht, which was tied to the US dollar, was under pressure as currency reserves fell. Despite rising indicators of fragility, herd behaviour kept investors engaged. International money continued to flow into the area, enticed by the 'Asian Miracle' myth. It was not just individuals; massive institutions and banks continued to invest, confident that they could leave the market before the collapse. But by July 1997, the burden was too significant. The Thai government was compelled to relinquish its dollar peg, enabling the baht to float. The currency rapidly fell by more than 50%, causing a domino effect across Asia.

The fall of the Thai baht was like a spark in a parched forest. Realising the possibility of similar flaws in other Asian economies, investors started a rapid flight. In Indonesia, the rupiah began to fall, shedding more than 80% of its value in only months. The Philippine peso, Malaysian ringgit, and South Korean won all followed suit as panic selling spread throughout the region. Stock markets crashed: the Jakarta Stock Exchange lost 75% of its value, while the Korea Composite Stock Price Index (KOSPI) fell 50%. Overnight, billions of dollars evaporated as foreign investors fled, withdrawing their funds from the area at a dizzying pace. What began as a promising growth story quickly devolved into a financial disaster.

The psychological reasons driving this fear are a textbook case of herding behaviour and the availability heuristic. Investors, unsure which economies might be harmed next, saw the whole region as a single risk, withdrawing from all Asian markets regardless of individual nation fundamentals. Fear supplanted analysis. News of one currency's depreciation became a signal to leave others, and the panic grew (DellaVigna, 2009). The Malaysian ringgit plunged by more than 45%, while the South Korean won lost half of its value. Investors, unaware of the facts but confident that the 'Asian Miracle' was finished, withdrew in droves, hastening the slump and exacerbating the catastrophe.

Speculative assaults on Asian currencies fuelled the flames. Hedge funds and significant investors saw a chance to profit and started shorting Asian currencies, wagering on their capacity to sustain stability. In Malaysia and the Philippines, central banks intervened by purchasing their currencies and defending exchange rates. However, these initiatives proved unsustainable. Malaysia's reserves decreased by more than 30% in a couple of months, and borrowing rates skyrocketed, further straining an already vulnerable economy. The speculative assaults showed no compassion, leaving governments fighting to stabilise their economies within a never-ending downward spiral.

In a frantic attempt to restore stability, the International Monetary Fund (IMF) intervened with emergency bailouts. South Korea, Thailand, and Indonesia got IMF packages worth about $40 billion, but the assistance came with onerous terms. Countries were forced to undertake austerity measures, such as decreasing government expenditure, hiking interest rates, and eliminating subsidies, in return for aid.

These policies, designed to establish budgetary restraint, had severe effects. In Indonesia, where the crisis had already resulted in high inflation and unemployment, austerity measures exacerbated economic hardship, causing significant demonstrations and social upheaval. President Suharto, who had controlled Indonesia for more than three decades, was forced to resign in 1998 due to rising widespread outrage.

The human toll of the catastrophe was enormous. Millions in Asia plunged into poverty as unemployment rose and companies shuttered. In Thailand, where the crisis originated, nearly 1 million jobs were lost in the first year alone, and the economy shrank by 10%. South Korea had its difficulties, with hundreds of enterprises going bankrupt and unemployment reaching 7.5%, a figure unprecedented in the area. Indonesia experienced the worst, with inflation exceeding 70% and poverty rates almost doubling, impacting millions of people (DellaVigna, 2009). Millions of people experienced a social, political, and profound personal crisis in addition to an economic one.

In the aftermath, Asia's economies were compelled to recover, but with prudence and a renewed understanding of the dangers of speculative debt and overreliance on foreign investment. Many governments tightened banking rules, enhanced transparency, and raised foreign reserves to prepare for future crises. South Korea's foreign currency reserves, for example, increased from $20 billion in 1997 to more than $400 billion in the 2010s, demonstrating the lessons learnt from the crisis.

Figure 6.1 clearly illustrates the stock market trends of Thailand (SET Index), Indonesia (Jakarta Composite Index), South Korea (KOSPI), and Malaysia (KLCI) during the Asian Financial Crisis. This graphic depiction illustrates the rapid

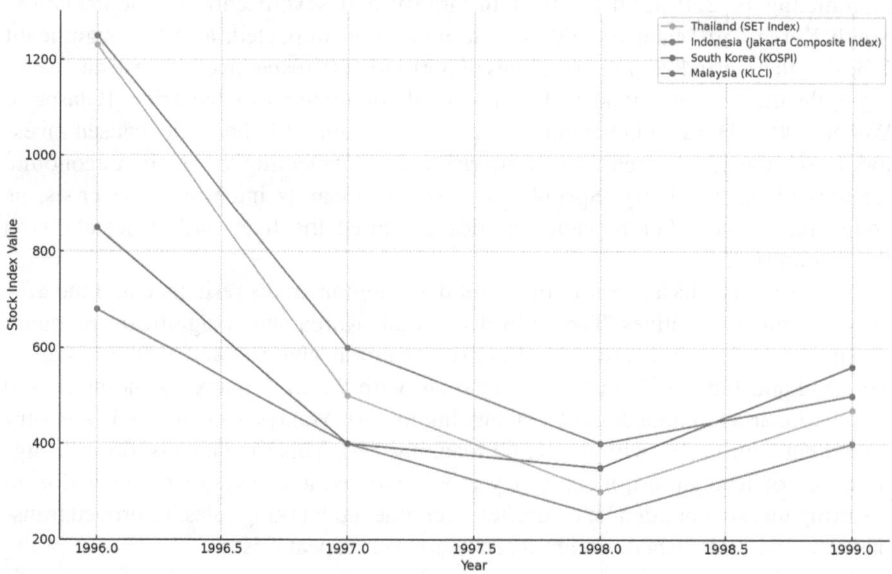

Fig. 6.1 Stock market performance during the Asian Financial Crisis (1996–1999)

deterioration of financial markets in various countries and emphasises their steady, if inconsistent, recovery after one of the most catastrophic financial crises in contemporary history.

In 1996, the stock indexes of these countries attained notable peaks, indicative of the confidence and enthusiasm linked to the 'Asian Miracle'. For instance, Thailand's SET Index and Malaysia's KLCI were recorded at 1230 and 1250, respectively, reflecting investor confidence driven by years of vigorous economic expansion and significant foreign investment. This era was the pinnacle of speculative behaviour, characterised by overconfidence bias that fuelled unrestrained capital inflows and hazardous lending practices. Foreign investors, captivated by the allure of perpetual wealth, invested heavily in these economies, failing to consider the structural weaknesses that underpinned their economic success.

The crisis started in 1997, instigated by the fall of the Thai baht. The SET Index plummeted below 500 as the currency depreciation revealed the vulnerability of Thailand's financial sector, significantly encumbered by foreign-denominated debt. The baht's depreciation served as a contagion catalyst, generating apprehension in adjacent markets. Investors, influenced by herd mentality, began major withdrawals from the area, exacerbating the financial instability. The graph illustrates a significant decrease in Indonesia's Jakarta Composite Index and South Korea's KOSPI, as both markets were adversely affected by the panic-driven capital outflow. The KLCI in Malaysia had a 50% decline in value as the ringgit encountered substantial pressure, illustrating the repercussions of regional interconnectedness.

By 1998, the crisis had to its nadir, as seen in Fig. 6.1. The SET Index of Thailand declined to 300, representing a significant 75% decrease from its pre-crisis zenith. Indonesia suffered even more dramatic losses, with its Jakarta Composite Index plummeting to 250 amid political instability and severe currency depreciation. South Korea and Malaysia, although less severely impacted, also had significant drops, with their indices reaching lows of 350 and 400, respectively. These decreases highlight the psychological and behavioural foundations of the crisis (Glaser & Weber, 2007). Herding behaviour, driven by the availability heuristic, caused investors to see the whole area as a single risk entity, neglecting the distinct economic realities of each country. Speculative currency assaults intensified the crisis, as hedge funds and other financial entities exploited the fear, further destabilising these countries.

The recovery phase, seen in the 1999 data, demonstrates resilience and the efficacy of policy initiatives. The KOSPI of South Korea saw a significant rebound, ascending to 560, indicative of effective structural changes and IMF assistance. Thailand and Indonesia started stabilisation, with the SET Index ascending to 470 and the Jakarta Composite Index enhancing to 400. Malaysia's comeback was very muted but significant, with the KLCI reaching 500. This time underscores the significance of foreign aid, local policy modifications, and investor re-evaluation in restoring market confidence. Countries strengthened banking rules, improved transparency, and replenished foreign reserves to avert repeat crises.

The Asian Financial Crisis serves as a sharp warning of the risks of overconfidence, speculative fervour, and herd behaviour in financial markets. The 'Asian

Miracle' was shown as a fiction constructed on shaky foundations, susceptible to psychological biases and collective behaviour that may destabilise economies. Behavioural finance tells us that markets are both psychological and economic. The crisis demonstrated that even the most promising growth stories may unravel in the face of rampant speculation and herd mentality, which substitutes critical analysis with blind optimism and panic.

6.3 2008 Subprime Mortgage Crisis: How Greed, Overconfidence, and Fear Brought Down the Financial System

The 2008 financial crisis was more than simply a market correction; it was a collapse that shook the foundations of global banking, revealing the flaws of a system predicated on reckless risk-taking, unrestrained greed, and naive optimism. The US housing market, long regarded to be secure and dependable, has devolved into a casino of speculation, overconfidence, and moral hazard. With mortgage brokers, investment banks, and homeowners all confident that property values could only rise, the financial system devolved into an ornate tower of cards, doomed to collapse (Hirshleifer & Shumway, 2003). And fall it did, leaving a trail of destruction that cost the global economy over $10 trillion in lost productivity, claimed millions of lives, and permanently altered our perception of financial risk.

The narrative starts in the early 2000s, when cheap interest rates, a housing boom, and an insatiable need for returns combined to create the perfect storm. Banks started providing mortgages to almost anybody who stepped in the door, bypassing conventional credit checks in favour of 'no-doc' and 'stated income' loans. Subprime lending—mortgages granted to customers with poor credit scores—exploded, increasing from $160 billion in 2001 to more than $600 billion by 2006. Investment banks and mortgage lenders were flush with cash. As demand for mortgages increased, lenders relaxed rules even further, providing adjustable-rate mortgages (ARMs) with low initial rates that would explode after a few years.

To fuel the boom, Wall Street produced two new types of financial products: mortgage-backed securities (MBS) and collateralised debt obligations (CDOs). These sophisticated instruments enabled banks to bundle thousands of mortgages, segment them into tranches, and offer them as securities to investors all over the world. By 2007, the MBS and CDO market had expanded to more than $7 trillion, with financial institutions, pension funds, and other large investors participating internationally (Glaser & Weber, 2007). These securities were lucrative, and the fees produced were enormous. Investment banks such as Lehman Brothers, Bear Stearns, and Merrill Lynch made billions by purchasing mortgages, packaging them into securities, and selling them off, sometimes with AAA ratings from credit rating agencies that underestimated—or ignored—the danger.

However, these good evaluations disguised a significant flaw: the system's financial incentives promoted risky behaviour. Known as a moral hazard, this tendency allowed lenders and banks to shift the risk of these loans to investors, relieving them of any actual responsibility. Mortgage originators needed more motivation to evaluate customers' creditworthiness since they sold the loans. The risk had transferred, but the benefits remained in their wallets. Homebuyers were also caught up in the excitement, taking out loans they could not pay in the long term. They were enticed by the promise of 'easy' homeownership, believing that property prices would continue to climb, allowing them to refinance or sell for a profit before their loan rates reset.

As property prices stabilised in 2006, fractures started to appear. As interest rates rose, borrowers who had taken out ARMs started to face larger monthly payments. By 2007, mortgage delinquencies were increasing at an alarming rate, particularly among subprime borrowers. In the second quarter of 2007, the default rate on subprime loans increased to 15.6%—a warning signal that many in the sector disregarded. The banks that owned MBS and CDOs were suddenly left with assets worth substantially less than they had expected. As defaults increased, the value of these assets fell, and financial institutions suffered massive losses.

By 2008, the crisis was in full swing. Bear Stearns, an investment bank heavily involved in mortgage-backed securities, failed in March and was purchased by JPMorgan Chase for $2 per share, a fraction of its previous worth. Lehman Brothers, another key participant in the MBS market, filed bankruptcy on September 15, 2008, in one of the most significant financial catastrophes in history. With $600 billion in assets, Lehman's bankruptcy sent shockwaves across global markets, signalling that the economic system was on the verge of collapse. Stock markets throughout the globe fell; by the end of 2008, the S&P 500 had lost about 40% of its value, wiping away billions of dollars in investor capital.

The problem was more comprehensive than the banks. It had a far-reaching impact on the economy, destroying towns and people. Home values fell by about 20% on average throughout the United States, with certain places such as Nevada, Florida, and Arizona reporting drops of 50% or more. Foreclosures have increased. In 2008 alone, there were 2.3 million foreclosure filings in the United States, and by 2010, more than 10 million homes had been lost to foreclosure. Entire neighbourhoods were hollowed out, and families who had bought into the promise of homeownership found themselves homeless or burdened with debt they could not pay off (Ben-David et al., 2013).

As fear spread, credit markets stopped. Banks, unclear of each other's exposure to bad debt, ceased lending, causing a credit crisis that brought enterprises to a halt. Small firms failed to get the capital they required to operate, resulting in widespread lay-offs and closures. Unemployment in the United States rose to 10% by October 2009, with more than 15 million people out of work. The economic agony expanded internationally, sending economies from Europe to Asia into recession and reducing global commerce by 12% in 2009—the most significant drop since World War II.

To halt the bleeding, governments and central banks undertook a series of extraordinary measures. The United States government approved the Troubled

Asset Relief Program (TARP), which authorised $700 billion to bail out failing banks and purchase hazardous assets. The Federal Reserve lowered interest rates to near-zero levels and implemented quantitative easing, buying government and mortgage bonds to pump cash into the economy. In sum, the Fed injected more than $4 trillion into the financial system, an unprecedented involvement. Overseas, the European Central Bank, Bank of England, and other institutions followed suit, implementing stimulus programmes and interest rate cuts to stabilise their economies.

The 2008 crisis showed the enormous hazards of unrestrained overconfidence, herd mentality, and moral hazard. It demonstrated how quickly investors, banks, and people may forsake logical thought in the quest for wealth (DellaVigna, 2009). The lessons were harsh, but they were clear: markets are susceptible to the biases and behaviours that influence human decisions. Financial exuberance may mislead even the most brilliant minds to the realities of risk. Still, moral hazard enables organisations to take on enormous risks, knowing that someone else would shoulder the burden.

In the years after, governments have attempted to avert another crisis of this size by enacting stricter financial laws, such as the Dodd-Frank Act in the United States, which aimed to reduce risky lending and increase bank monitoring. The crisis had a significant and long-term effect on the global economy, reshaping the financial landscape. It showed us that the pursuit of profit, when unrestrained, can lead to disaster and that a sophisticated economic system founded on trust may collapse overnight if that trust is violated.

The 2008 financial crisis is more than just a cautionary story; it is a harsh reminder of the power and dangers of human behaviour in markets. It demonstrated that, although financial tools and technology change, human psychology stays consistent. Greed, fear, and overconfidence continue to destabilise economies, and history may repeat itself if vigilance and responsibility are not maintained.

6.4 Bitcoin Boom and Bust Cycles: A Modern Speculative Frenzy

Bitcoin, a mystery digital currency launched in 2009, has fascinated the globe like no other financial asset. Bitcoin, long a fringe notion supported by computer enthusiasts and libertarians, swiftly attracted public attention, igniting waves of speculative frenzy that turned it from a niche currency to a worldwide financial phenomenon. Bitcoin, which promised decentralisation, anonymity, and independence from government control, was heralded as the money of the future, an inflation hedge, and a revolutionary financial instrument. However, with each spectacular ascent comes a stunning collapse, as Bitcoin's boom and bust cycles have captivated—and devastated—investors throughout the globe.

Bitcoin's first substantial price increase occurred between 2011 and 2013 when it jumped from under $1 to more than $1000. Early adopters saw their holdings rise, becoming 'Bitcoin millionaires' almost immediately. By the time Bitcoin reached $20,000 in late 2017, it had become worldwide news. Media sources broadcast tales of ordinary individuals converting tiny investments into millionaires, and the public's interest in Bitcoin grew (Boutros et al., 2020). Mainstream investors and institutions started to buy in, motivated by recency bias—the notion that previous profits will continue eternally. Bitcoin was no longer a curiosity; it was an asset that everyone desired, a ticket to enormous riches.

The 2017 spike was a classic example of speculative exuberance. Investors rushed into Bitcoin without comprehending blockchain technology or the currency's limits. They were motivated by FOMO, worried they would miss out on the 'next big thing'. People who had never invested in digital currencies hopped on board, hoping to profit from what seemed to be an unstoppable trend. The Bitcoin mania was so severe that some people took out loans to enter the market, believing that their investment would only rise. However, in early 2018, the bubble popped. Bitcoin fell from about $20,000 to roughly $3000 in a few months, wiping billions of dollars in value and leaving many investors with significant losses.

The cycle repeated in 2020 and 2021, with Bitcoin hitting new highs, including $64,000 in April 2021. Thanks to high-profile endorsements, institutional involvement, and even comments from Tesla CEO Elon Musk, Bitcoin seemed unstoppable. However, as has been the case in the past, the thrill was fleeting. By mid-2021, Bitcoin's price had fallen to roughly $30,000, highlighting the currency's tremendous volatility and warning investors of the fine line between boom and disaster (Loang, 2024).

The adaptive market hypothesis provides a persuasive framework for analysing Bitcoin's severe cycles. According to economist Andrew Lo, markets are like ecosystems that continually adapt to new players and information. As Bitcoin has developed, it has attracted a broader spectrum of investors, from amateur enthusiasts to institutional powerhouses. Each new cycle introduces new participants, trade behaviours, and ambitions, resulting in constantly shifting dynamics. What was once a tiny market for computer specialists has grown into a worldwide asset class. Still, the boom and bust cycles continue as new investors join with their prejudices and preconceptions.

Bitcoin's volatility is worsened by its uncontrolled status. Unlike conventional assets, Bitcoin is not dependent on economic fundamentals or central bank policy. Its price is almost entirely determined by mood, hype, and communal belief (Königstorfer & Thalmann, 2020). Social media platforms play an essential role, with each tweet or headline sending tremors across the market. During bull markets, optimism is infectious; during downturns, dread spreads as swiftly. Bitcoin's price swings often mirror this feeling, rising and decreasing with the aggregate emotions of investors throughout the globe.

Every Bitcoin cycle reminds us of the psychological reasons that drive speculative markets. Recency bias leads investors to believe that since Bitcoin has lately performed well, it will continue to do so (Statman, 2017). However, as each cycle demonstrates, the truth is far more complicated. Those that purchase during the excitement often sell at a loss after the bubble collapses. Bitcoin's tale is still unfolding, but its booms and busts have cemented its status as a high-stakes game of psychological endurance.

Bitcoin's history is similar to the cautionary tale of Tulip Mania, which illustrates how speculative bubbles emerge, fuelled by emotion and popular belief. It demonstrates that, despite technological advancements, human psychology remains primarily unchanged. The desire for money, the thrill of speculation, and the naive hope that 'this time is different' continue to drive markets, making Bitcoin a timeless representation of both the promise and risk of speculation.

6.5 COVID-19 Pandemic Market Crash and Recovery: The Psychology of Panic and Resilience

In early 2020, the world altered very instantly. News of a mystery virus spreading in China sparked a worldwide catastrophe as COVID-19 swept across nations, causing lockdowns, stopping companies, and suspending travel. Markets, which had been soaring, were thrown into disarray. Fear and uncertainty gripped investors as they confronted an unprecedented danger to the global economy. What followed was one of the most rapid and severe stock market collapses in history, demonstrating the importance of investor panic, loss aversion, and adaptive herding behaviour as psychological factors driving market dynamics.

As the pandemic's consequences became apparent, investors were overcome with a terrible feeling of vulnerability. The S&P 500 fell 34% from its February peak to its March low, one of the worst declines in history. The Dow Jones Industrial Average saw its most significant single-day point decline in history on March 16, shedding 2997 points. This tremendous sell-off was not motivated by conventional financial principles but by pure panic. Investors rushed to sell assets, preferring cash to equities, anticipating a worldwide economic disaster. This massive flight is explained by behavioural finance as loss aversion, a significant bias in which the pain of possible losses surpasses the desire for future rewards. Faced with an uncertain future, investors were eager to sell at any price, motivated by the need to save all they could.

Panic quickly spread, and herding behaviour fuelled the selling frenzy. In the lack of clear information, investors looked to one another, mimicking the conduct of people around them in a concerted effort to limit risk. This adaptive herding was seen not just among individual investors but also among institutional participants, as even experienced investors responded to market mood (Liu et al., 2020). With each sale, the sense of danger grew, fuelling a vicious cycle of fear and more excellent selling. Fear was heightened by social media and news sites, which were full of grim forecasts and constant updates. Headlines blared with terminology like 'recession', 'depression', and 'market collapse', adding fuel to the flames and making the danger seem all-encompassing.

However, when markets spiralled, governments throughout the globe adopted extreme steps to stabilise the economy. In the United States, Congress enacted the $2 trillion CARES Act in March 2020, which includes direct payments to people, loans for small companies, and assistance for affected sectors. The Federal Reserve cut interest rates to near-zero levels and implemented emergency lending initiatives. Similar interventions were conducted across the world, with central banks and governments stepping in to avert a financial collapse. These initiatives constituted a tipping point, as market attitude gradually shifted from fear to cautious optimism.

Loss aversion, which first drove the enormous exodus from equities, is now a factor in the rush to re-enter the market. Investors, fearful of missing out on the bounce, started buying back in, anxious to capitalise on the recovery gains. This change from fear-driven selling to optimism-driven purchasing revealed sentiment's ability to both push markets down and pull them back up. The pandemic's market rebound demonstrated how investor psychology can shift quickly, adjusting to new facts and changing expectations as situations change.

Figure 6.2 captures the dramatic trajectory of the S&P 500 Index during the early months of the COVID-19 pandemic, offering a visual narrative of the psychological and behavioural forces that influenced market dynamics. This performance vividly illustrates the interplay of fear, uncertainty, and adaptive decision-making among investors as they grappled with an unprecedented global crisis.

At the onset of 2020, markets were riding a wave of confidence, reflected in the S&P 500's peak in February. Investor sentiment at this stage was buoyant, underpinned by strong economic indicators and optimism regarding continued growth. Behavioural tendencies such as overconfidence played a significant role in

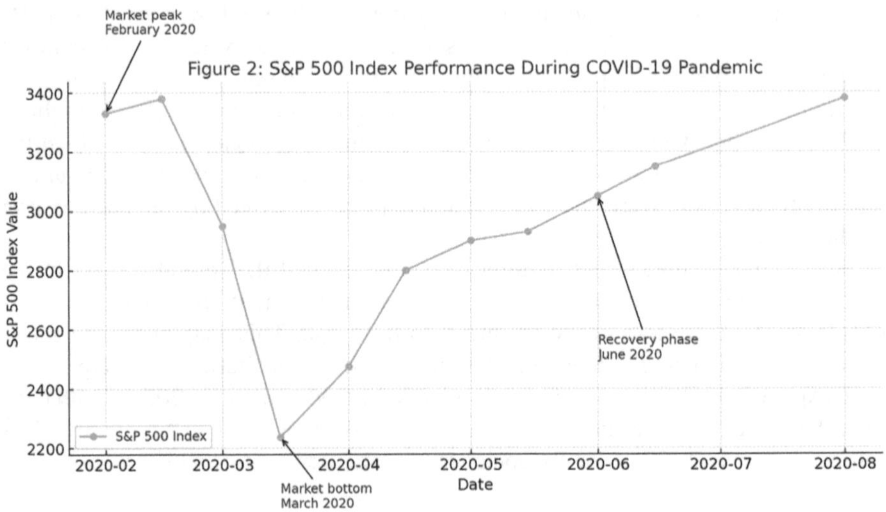

Fig. 6.2 S&P 500 Index performance during the COVID-19 pandemic

maintaining this market exuberance. Despite emerging reports of a novel virus in China, there was little indication in market behaviour of the seismic disruptions that were to follow. Investors largely discounted the potential economic impact of the virus, illustrating a common behavioural bias where individuals underestimate low-probability but high-impact events.

The transition from confidence to panic was abrupt. As COVID-19 cases surged globally and nations implemented strict lockdown measures, markets reacted with unprecedented speed. By March 2020, the S&P 500 had fallen 34% from its Februarys. This collapse, one of the most rapid in history, highlights the dominance of emotional reactions during periods of crisis. The concept of loss aversion is central to understanding this phase. Investors, driven by the pain of potential financial losses, engaged in mass selling to preserve what they could, often at steep discounts. The decision to liquidate assets was not rooted in rational evaluations of intrinsic value but in a deep psychological need to avoid further losses. This behaviour reflects a core tenet of behavioural finance: the asymmetry in how individuals perceive gains and losses, with losses eliciting far stronger emotional reactions.

The widespread panic triggered herding behaviour, as uncertainty prompted investors to look to others for cues. In the absence of clear information, market participants, including institutional investors, mimicked the actions of their peers in an effort to limit perceived risks. This herding behaviour exacerbated the sell-off, creating a self-reinforcing cycle where each wave of selling deepened fears and drove additional liquidation. Social media and news outlets amplified this phenomenon, with dire headlines emphasising recessionary risks and economic collapse. The psychological impact of such messaging cannot be overstated, as it heightened a collective sense of urgency and reinforced the perception of imminent disaster.

Despite the severity of the downturn, Fig. 6.2 also demonstrates the resilience and adaptability of markets in the face of adversity. By April, unprecedented government interventions began to shift market sentiment. The $2 trillion CARES Act in the United States, along with similar measures globally, injected liquidity into the economy and provided a safety net for businesses and individuals. The Federal Reserve's aggressive interest rate cuts and emergency lending programmes further bolstered confidence. These actions represent a critical turning point, as investors started to reassess the scale of the economic response and its implications for market stability.

The recovery, as depicted in the figure, was remarkably swift, with the S&P 500 regaining much of its losses by June and achieving pre-pandemic levels by August. This V-shaped recovery defied traditional expectations of prolonged economic stagnation and highlights the principles of the adaptive market hypothesis. Investors rapidly processed new information about fiscal and monetary support, leading to a shift in behaviour from panic-driven selling to optimism-fuelled buying. Loss aversion, which had initially driven the exodus from equities, now played a role in the recovery, as investors sought to re-enter the market to avoid missing out on potential gains (Boutros et al., 2020). This fear of missing out, combined with a perception of stabilising conditions, spurred a reversal in herding behaviour, with investors collectively driving market prices higher.

The COVID-19 pandemic's influence on financial markets illustrated the intricate interplay of fear, hope, and resilience. It was a case study of how rapidly market sentiment may alter in the face of an unexpected catastrophe, calling into question the concept that markets are exclusively rational. The first crisis demonstrated the power of fear and herd mentality, yet the quick rebound demonstrated the market's capacity to adapt and even flourish under extreme situations. The epidemic taught investors a valuable lesson in behavioural finance, emphasising the need to understand not just economic data but also the emotional impulses that drive markets.

The financial crises discussed in this chapter serve as stark reminders that markets, no matter how sophisticated, are fundamentally human constructions. History's crashes and collapses show a pattern of psychological pitfalls—overconfidence that leads to despair, herding behaviour that fuels booms and busts, and loss aversion that exacerbates panic. Each crisis tells a similar story: markets are never entirely logical, and when feeling, emotion, and belief take over, financial stability deteriorates (Hirshleifer, 2015).

As we go ahead, these teachings are as vital as ever. Behavioural finance demonstrates that without knowledge of our personal biases and a framework to protect against collective irrationality, we risk repeating the same errors. The objective is not to eradicate human behaviour from finance but rather to comprehend it, recognise warning signals, and develop resilience in an uncertain environment. Each crisis provides an opportunity to learn and adapt, ensuring that we not only survive financial turmoil but also emerge more innovative as a result of it.

References

Ackert, L. F., & Deaves, R. (2009). *Behavioral finance: Psychology, decision-making, and markets*. South-Western Cengage Learning.

Ben-David, I. T. Z. H. A. K., Franzoni, F., Landier, A., & Moussawi, R. (2013). Do hedge funds manipulate stock prices? *The Journal of Finance, 68*(6), 2383–2434.

Boutros, M., Ben-David, I., Graham, J. R., Harvey, C. R., & Payne, J. W. (2020). *The persistence of miscalibration*. National Bureau of Economic Research.

Camerer, C. F., & Loewenstein, G. (2004). Behavioral economics: Past, present, and future. In *Advances in behavioral economics* (pp. 3–51). Princeton University Press.

Daniel, K., Hirshleifer, D., & Subrahmanyam, A. (1998). Investor psychology and security market under-and overreactions. *The Journal of Finance, 53*(6), 1839–1885.

DellaVigna, S. (2009). Psychology and economics: Evidence from the field. *Journal of Economic Literature, 47*(2), 315–372.

Glaser, M., & Weber, M. (2007). Overconfidence and trading volume. *The Geneva Risk and Insurance Review, 32*, 1–36.

Hirshleifer, D. (2015). The psychology of financial decision-making. *Annual Review of Financial Economics, 7*(1), 133–159.

Hirshleifer, D., & Shumway, T. (2003). Good day sunshine: Stock returns and the weather. *The Journal of Finance, 58*(3), 1009–1032.

Königstorfer, F., & Thalmann, S. (2020). Applications of Artificial Intelligence in commercial banks–A research agenda for behavioral finance. *Journal of Behavioral and Experimental Finance, 27*, 100352.

Liu, Y., Sun, Q., & Wu, L. (2020). Sentiment-based investment strategies: A machine learning perspective. *Journal of Behavioral Finance, 21*(4), 341–359.

Lo, A. W. (2004). Adaptive markets: A financial evolutionary theory. *Journal of Portfolio Management, 30*(5), 15–29.

Loang, O. K. (2024). Stability of Shariah-compliant stocks in Indonesia, Malaysia, and Gcc: The roles of monetary and fiscal policies and contagion. *Journal of Islamic Monetary Economics and Finance, 10*(1), 155–176.

Malmendier, U., & Nagel, S. (2011). Depression babies: Do macroeconomic experiences affect risk-taking? *The Quarterly Journal of Economics, 126*(1), 373–416.

Odean, T. (1998). Are investors reluctant to realize their losses? *The Journal of Finance, 53*(5), 1775–1798.

Raimundo Júnior, G. D. S., Palazzi, R. B., Tavares, R. D. S., & Klotzle, M. C. (2022). Market stress and herding: A new approach to the cryptocurrency market. *Journal of Behavioral Finance, 23*(1), 43–57.

Shiller, R. J. (2000). *Irrational exuberance*. Princeton University Press.

Statman, M. (2017). *Finance for normal people: How investors and markets behave*. Oxford University Press.

Thaler, R. H., & Sunstein, C. R. (2008). *Nudge: Improving decisions about health, wealth, and happiness*. Penguin Books.

Wermers, R. (1999). Mutual fund herding and its impact on stock prices. *The Journal of Finance, 54*(2), 581–622.

Chapter 7
Psychological Drivers of Stock Market Behaviour

In the realm of finance, the stock market is often seen as a haven of rational decision-making—a place where investors analyse data, evaluate risks, and act on logical projections. However, everyone who has seen a market rally rise or a fall unravel understands that underlying every move is something considerably more complex: human psychology. Stocks do not rise and fall just on the basis of balance sheets and earnings reports; they are also influenced by a powerful combination of fear, greed, hope, and, in some cases, pure stubbornness. These psychological influences influence every transaction, influencing patterns, creating bubbles, and producing severe sell-offs. The stock market is, in many respects, a reflection of our collective emotions, heightened by the enormous amount of people, information, and money that passes through it.

This chapter investigates the psychological factors that influence—and often misguide—investor behaviour (Glaser & Weber, 2007). These psychological effects, ranging from the draw of conformity to the pull of overconfidence, may transform rational markets into unexpected environments. Understanding these factors entails more than simply recognising why investors behave in specific ways; it also entails identifying the underlying patterns that might lead to excessive exuberance, panic, or even market-wide declines. Exploring these behavioural undercurrents helps us understand why stock prices often defy rationality and why market 'sentiment' is just as important as market facts. This voyage into the psychology of stock market behaviour illustrates that, although markets may seem to be statistics and charts, they are fundamentally driven by the human mind.

Table 7.1 outlines the psychological key drivers of stock market behaviour. The stock market, often considered a domain of rational analysis and data-driven decision-making, is profoundly influenced by human psychology. Fear and greed emerge as powerful forces driving market volatility. In times of uncertainty, fear prompts investors to sell en masse, prioritising the avoidance of potential losses over rational analysis. Conversely, during bull markets, greed takes centre stage, with investors driven by the allure of rapid gains. This duality fuels cycles of panic

K. L. Ooi, *Demystifying Behavioral Finance*,
https://doi.org/10.1007/978-981-96-2690-8_7

Table 7.1 Psychological drivers of stock market behaviour

Key psychological drivers	Description	Impact on stock market behaviour
Fear and greed	Emotions that dominate during uncertainty or opportunity	Fear causes panic selling, while greed drives speculative buying, creating volatility and market inefficiencies
Loss aversion	A bias where losses are felt more deeply than equivalent gains	Leads to irrational selling during downturns and mispricing of risk
Herd behaviour	The tendency to mimic the actions of others in uncertain situations	Amplifies market movements, contributing to bubbles and crashes as investors collectively follow trends without analysis
Overconfidence	Excessive belief in one's own knowledge or predictive abilities	Results in risky trading behaviours, excessive speculation, and dismissal of contrary evidence
Fear of missing out	Anxiety of being left out when others are perceived to be gaining	Prompts hasty investment decisions, inflating bubbles as investors rush to join trends
Adaptive herding	Shifting behaviour based on new information or observed actions of others	Explains rapid market shifts during crises or recovery phases, driven by collective reinterpretation of market signals

selling and speculative buying, disrupting market stability and challenging the traditional notion of efficient markets. Loss aversion further deepens the psychological impact on financial decisions (Hirshleifer & Shumway, 2003). This bias, which reflects the tendency to weigh potential losses more heavily than equivalent gains, often leads to irrational behaviour. Investors may cling to losing investments in hopes of recovery or exit profitable positions prematurely to lock in gains. In broader market contexts, loss aversion exacerbates downturns, as fear of further losses drives selling even when fundamentals suggest otherwise.

Herd behaviour is another critical factor, particularly in uncertain or rapidly changing market conditions. Investors often look to others for cues, assuming that collective actions reflect superior information or strategies. This behaviour creates self-reinforcing cycles, where trends gain momentum irrespective of their fundamental justification. The result is often the formation of speculative bubbles, followed by sharp corrections when the collective belief system collapses (Glaser & Weber, 2007). Overconfidence adds another layer of complexity. This bias leads investors to overestimate their knowledge or predictive abilities, often resulting in excessive trading, speculative risk-taking, and the dismissal of warnings or contrary evidence. Overconfidence not only distorts individual portfolios but also contributes to market-wide exuberance or neglect.

Fear of missing out, a more contemporary phenomenon magnified by social media and hyperconnectivity, underscores the urgency investors feel to participate in perceived opportunities. The anxiety of being left out propels investors to act impulsively, fueling asset price inflation and intensifying speculative cycles. FOMO played a notable role in events like the GameStop saga, where retail investors rushed to capitalise on perceived gains, often disregarding risk. Adaptive herding describes the dynamic shifts in collective behaviour as new information emerges. Unlike traditional herding, adaptive herding reflects a conscious adjustment to perceived signals, such as government interventions or corporate announcements. This phenomenon was evident during the COVID-19 pandemic, where initial panic-driven selling transitioned to optimism as stimulus measures were announced, demonstrating the market's ability to adapt rapidly to evolving circumstances.

7.1 FOMO: The Relentless Pursuit of the Next Big Thing

Nothing quite like FOMO, or fear of missing out, can convert even the most careful investor into a risk-taker. It's an emotional tsunami that strikes when we watch people around us profiting, celebrating, and seizing the elusive 'next big thing'. Suddenly, logical thought takes a back seat, and the desire to join in on the activity becomes overpowering. It's more than a drive for profit; it's the highly uncomfortable sensation of being left behind, of seeing opportunity slip away while everyone else seems to be cashing in. And at such times FOMO is more than a whisper; it's a scream that drowns out analysis and heightens urgency.

The cryptocurrency markets are the best illustration of FOMO at their peak. When Bitcoin surged in 2017, many who'd never heard of blockchain rushed to become involved, believing they were seeing a revolution they couldn't afford to miss. As Bitcoin's price rose from around $1000 to almost $20,000 in less than a year, fear of missing out spread widely. Dinner parties, office banter, and family gatherings all became venues for individuals to share tales about how much they'd earned or wanted to make. Then, there were some on the sidelines, watching in jealousy and feeling the agony of missed opportunities. The frenzy was not about knowing the technology or the foundations but about getting in on the action before it was 'too late'.

For many, 'too late' arrived far sooner than they imagined. When Bitcoin's price fell below $7000 only months later, thousands of new investors were left with assets that had swiftly lost value. FOMO had pushed them in at top prices, and the market's sharp drop left them with significant losses. According to a 2020 survey, more than 60% of crypto investors acknowledged investing out of fear of losing out rather than because they believed in the long-term potential. FOMO does more than only motivate us to pursue gains; it also convinces us that we are running out of time to claim what is appropriately ours, producing a feeling of urgency that leaves little space for reason (Raimundo Júnior et al., 2022).

However, FOMO is not unique to the cryptocurrency sector; it appears in every financial bubble, from the tulip craze of the 1600s to the dot-com boom of the late 1990s. During the housing boom that preceded 2008, for example, people waited up outside open houses, bidding wars broke out, and properties sold for far more than the asking price. What's the logic? If you don't purchase now, you'll never get in. As a result, many who couldn't afford it overspent, investing in an unstoppable market. When the market broke, FOMO caused financial misery, leaving numerous homeowners with houses worth less than their mortgages. FOMO affects not just investors but also families, communities, and economies, transforming reasonable planning into speculative hysteria.

Social media has further exacerbated the hold of FOMO, altering how we perceive and respond to market trends. Stories of 10x gains and overnight millionaires abound on sites such as Twitter, Reddit, and Instagram, creating an echo chamber that promotes FOMO at unprecedented rates and scale. Now, a single tweet or viral article may bring hundreds racing to purchase a stock, causing price increases based on nothing more than digital excitement. The 2021 'meme stock' frenzy, in which GameStop and AMC shares skyrocketed owing to social media buzz, demonstrated how intense FOMO can be in today's digital era. Retail investors flocked into equities not because of their fundamentals but because they wanted to be a part of a movement and were afraid of missing out as others profited.

The irony of FOMO-driven investment is that it generally peaks precisely as the market is about to shift. By the time most people are hurrying to purchase, the 'smart money' has already left, leaving latecomers carrying the bag. Research backs this up: studies indicate that FOMO-driven investments generally underperform the market since they are done hastily and with minimal due research. According to a 2019 poll, more than 70% of investors who acted on FOMO acknowledged needing to do more research instead of relying on hype and rumour. Finally, FOMO may be financially catastrophic, driving individuals to seek profits that were never there in the first place, all while disregarding warning flags that they might have recognised if they had taken a step back.

The most damaging aspect of FOMO is that it completely changes our attitude towards investing. It replaces strategy with instinct and patience with a rush. When we're experiencing FOMO, every new news or market move seems enormous, indicating that action must be made quickly. FOMO not only makes us want to invest; it also makes us feel compelled to do so since staying on the sidelines means missing out (Baek & Lee, 2021). It affects the investor's psyche, transforming meticulous planners into gamblers and diligent savers into speculators. Discipline is frequently the difference between gaining money and losing it in the world of investing. Still, FOMO undermines discipline by encouraging us to make choices based on our fears rather than our aspirations.

FOMO emphasises the necessity of self-awareness and control. Markets are naturally cyclical, possibilities are limitless, and missing one does not imply missing them all. The greatest investors learn to recognise when FOMO is in control, taking a step back to remind themselves that the stock market values patience and analysis above impulsive decisions. In a society where we are continuously bombarded with success tales, it is tempting to assume that if we do not act now, we will never have another opportunity. But the fact is that there will always be another chance or market shift. The actual problem is understanding when to ignore the noise, believe in your approach, and remember that sometimes the most excellent way to win is to avoid playing the game that everyone else is rushing into.

7.2 Overconfidence Bias: The Thrill of Playing the Market God

Imagine walking onto the stock market stage feeling like a master strategist, sure that you have it all figured out. Overconfidence is the surge of adrenaline that convinces you that every deal will be profitable and that every move you make is wiser, sharper, and destined for greatness. It's an investor's biggest delusion, motivating them to take ever-riskier bets and making the market seem like a stage designed just for them. Overconfident investors don't merely participate; they rejoice, believing that every dollar invested is the beginning of something great. But there's a catch: overconfidence is both blinding and exhilarating.

Overconfidence bias was at its peak during the late 1990s dot-com boom. Investors flocked to Internet equities as if every business with '.com' in its name was the next Microsoft. Companies with no profitability and few goods get billion-dollar values. Qualcomm, one of the hottest tech companies, had its price increase by 2619% in only 1 year. People stopped verifying foundations and asking questions; they just wanted in. Everyone, from experienced traders to day traders, believed they could predict the next big winner. But as the bubble broke, reality struck hard. Markets fell by 78% in certain areas, and fortunes that seemed inevitable disappeared suddenly. Overconfidence had built a dream world of invincibility, and the fall dragged every single believer back to reality.

Overconfidence not only causes faulty judgements but also creates a trading frenzy. According to research, overconfident investors trade 50% more often than others, sure that each transaction would result in higher earnings. However, their average yearly returns are usually 11% lower than those who trade less, resulting in significantly more losses than gains while attempting to play the hero. Each successful transaction perpetuates the cycle, creating a fortress of self-belief that shields investors from danger. Losses? They are tossed aside as 'flukes'. Successes? Proof that they are unique. However, the market has a way of humbling even the most arrogant players, proving that success in investing is seldom about bravado—it's about understanding when to back off.

The terrible reality about overconfidence is that it can create or shatter fortunes. It's like walking a tightrope with the audience applauding below; sure, you'll never fall. The stories of the dot-com millionaires who lost everything are cautionary tales of optimism turned disaster. What's the true lesson? The market values humility over arrogance and patience over pride. In the realm of investment, the pleasure of overconfidence is transitory, while underestimating danger may be disastrous.

7.3 Herd Behaviour: Following the Crowd to Fortune—or Folly

Herd behaviour in the stock market is more than simply a quirk; it's a gravitational force that draws investors to the safety of the crowd. It's a strong impulse that stems from our evolutionary history when safety was generally found in large groups. When investors see others flocking to a hot stock, the desire to follow in might be overpowering. Why stand out when everyone else seems to be cashing in? The market now seems safer, as if the crowd had some hidden wisdom that makes everything failsafe. However, when herd behaviour takes hold, equities rise and fall on emotion, resulting in violent waves of volatility.

In 2021, herd behaviour went viral. Social media sites such as Reddit's WallStreetBets helped GameStop and AMC become household names. Fuelled by tweets and Reddit postings, GameStop's stock skyrocketed over 1700% in only 1 month, converting the ailing business into a cultural sensation. People invested not because they believed in the company's long-term prospects but because the audience was ecstatic. It was thrilling, an opportunity to challenge Wall Street itself. However, as the buzz dissipated, latecomers found themselves holding the bag. Prices plummeted, and riches vanished as swiftly as they emerged. Herd behaviour fuelled a speculative frenzy, luring individuals in with the promise of quick money—and leaving them with enormous losses.

Why do investors follow the herd? It's about surviving and assuming that if everyone else is doing it, it must be the best option. Herd behaviour makes investors more comfortable taking risks they would otherwise shun. It may intensify rallies, propelling stocks to stratospheric heights, but it can also instil fear, resulting in enormous sell-offs at the first indication of danger. According to behavioural finance studies, herding accounts for up to 60% of stock market volatility, transforming rational investment choices into irrational emotional responses. Herding provides the appearance of protection, yet it is a trap. When the throng moves, it might be challenging to resist, but if the momentum switches, the fall is harsh and cruel.

Investors who survive the market realise that the comfort of the herd is sometimes an illusion. While herding may provide short-term benefits, it seldom results in long-term success. The main issue is resisting the attraction, recognising when to stand apart, and remembering that in the stock market, following the crowd may sometimes lead to disaster.

7.4 Loss Aversion: The High Price of Playing It Safe

Loss aversion is more than simply a prejudice; it is a driving force that influences every investment choice. According to behavioural finance, losses have doubled the emotional weight of similar profits. In the stock market, investors' basic fear of loss may lead them to do the unthinkable: cling to losses, sell wins too soon, and take frantic measures to prevent additional agony. Loss aversion transforms the market into nerve-racking warfare, with every drop seeming like a dive and every recovery providing only short solace.

The 2008 financial crisis provided a crash education in loss aversion. As stock markets crashed and portfolios dwindled, investors tried to avoid the devastation. Trillions of dollars were lost in only a few months, and many people panicked and liquidated their possessions. According to studies, one out of every four investors sold their whole holdings, missing out on the subsequent rebound. The dread of future losses grew overwhelming, forcing them to forsake assets that, if kept on, would have recouped value. Loss aversion not only causes terrible judgements, but it may also lead to panic selling and impulsive behaviour, transforming brief losses into lifelong financial scars.

Loss aversion traps investors in what economists term the 'disposition effect'. They hold onto losing stocks, waiting for a recovery while selling winners to 'lock in gains'. A survey of broking accounts found that investors are 50% more likely to sell winning stocks than losing ones. This behaviour results in portfolios that underperform because investors need help keeping laggards while selling their best assets too soon. Loss aversion is more than simply avoiding discomfort; it is a deep, visceral urge to feel safe, even if it means giving up long-term advantages.

According to behavioural finance, loss aversion may distort a portfolio, resulting in a defensive approach that protects against short-term losses while sacrificing future potential. True resilience in the stock market comes from handling losses properly rather than avoiding them altogether. Loss aversion may lead investors to play it safe, but the cost of this protection is often more than they realise. The actual problem is learning to bear the pain, accept losses as part of the game, and invest with a clear, long-term perspective.

7.5 Confirmation Bias: Crafting Reality to Fit Your Beliefs

Confirmation bias is the propensity to perceive just what we want to see, filtering information so that it confirms our own opinions. It is a tremendous force in the stock market, producing an echo chamber in which every bit of favourable news seems to verify that an investment is the correct one. Confirmation bias creates a selective reality for investors, in which risks are minimised, warnings are disregarded, and optimism reigns supreme—even when the evidence indicates caution.

Consider the instance of Tesla. For many investors, Tesla is more than simply a vehicle firm; it's a vision for the future (Boutros et al., 2020). Those who believe in Tesla's goal see every record sale and new model as a boost to their confidence, while worries about valuation, competition, and regulatory challenges are discounted. This selective filtering creates an environment in which Tesla's success is seen as inevitable, blinding investors to possible hurdles. When a stock becomes more than an investment—when it becomes a belief—confirmation bias kicks in, and logical analysis takes a back seat.

The housing bubble of the early 2000s was another example of confirmation bias. Investors, homeowners, and banks all agreed that real estate prices could only rise. Dissenting voices were labelled as pessimists, and each new high was seen as proof that the boom would continue indefinitely. However, as the bubble burst, the illusion dissipated, leaving millions in financial misery. Confirmation bias affects more than simply individual portfolios; it can influence whole markets, producing settings in which disagreement is disregarded, and warnings are discounted as noise.

Confirmation bias causes investors to maintain holdings for longer than necessary. It results in imbalanced portfolios, which are weighted on companies that suit a particular narrative but need more diversity. According to behavioural finance research, more than 80% of investors seek information that supports their beliefs, resulting in portfolios built on hope rather than realities. The actual expertise in investing is in questioning our preconceptions, searching out facts that contradict our ideas, and understanding that being correct often means being uncomfortable. In the realm of investment, confirmation bias is a comforting blanket, but it can also be a trap.

7.6 Recency Bias: Living and Investing

Recency bias is the tendency to overemphasise the most recent occurrences as if the market's previous move is its only move. It's a mentality that persuades investors that whatever occurred yesterday will definitely happen tomorrow. When markets are rising, recency bias makes investors feel invincible; when they are dropping, it causes panic. This bias makes every rally seem like a boom and every decline feel like a disaster, encouraging investors to focus their choices on short-term fluctuations rather than long-term strategy.

Recency bias became prevalent in early 2020 as COVID-19 worries swept the globe. Investors saw the market plummet and assumed it would only worsen. Many others liquidated their assets to avert additional losses, confident that the slump would last. However, once the market recovered, several of these same investors hurried to reinvest, believing the recovery would be as long-lasting as the drop had been. This back-and-forth left them with the 'buy high, sell low' problem, fuelled by the emotional highs and lows of recent market fluctuations.

High-growth industries, such as technology, are ideal breeding grounds for recency bias. When Apple or Amazon's stock prices rise, investors believe that the trend will continue eternally. However, when a correction occurs, the same bias informs them that the drop will endure forever, causing them to depart prematurely. According to behavioural finance research, more than 60% of investors base their choices on current market movements rather than strategy, succumbing to short-term thinking that may disrupt even the best-laid plans.

Recency bias is a significant influence that clever investors learn to avoid. The market's most recent move is seldom its last one, and those who succeed look past today's headlines, basing their approach on a long-term perspective (DellaVigna & Pollet, 2009). Recency bias may make every downturn seem like a tragedy in the realm of investing, but genuine winners are those who maintain their eyes on the broad picture.

As we wrap up our investigation into the psychological causes of investor behaviour, it's apparent that the stock market is more than simply a field of data and graphs—it's a huge stage where human nature is on the whole show. Overconfidence, herd behaviour, loss aversion, confirmation bias, and recency bias all play a part, resulting in a landscape that is as much about feeling as analysis. These biases affect the market's every twist and turn, propelling us towards choices that may seem sensible in the time but show their actual character only in retrospect. In this context, investment becomes more than simply a financial decision; it becomes personal, even intensely emotional, impacted by invisible forces in our thoughts.

These psychological factors affect more than just individual investors; they also influence whole markets and economies. The dot-com bubble, the 2008 financial crisis, and cryptocurrency surges were more than simply financial occurrences; they were human tales formed by our innermost aspirations, fears, and biases. It's the joy of joining the crowd, the pain of a loss, the solace of hanging onto beliefs, and the dread of missing out. Each move we make, impacted by these biases, contributes to the narrative of the market, resulting in the boom-and-bust cycles that characterise our financial history.

References

Ackert, L. F., & Deaves, R. (2009). *Behavioral finance: Psychology, decision-making, and markets*. South-Western Cengage Learning.

An, L., Wang, H., Wang, J., & Yu, J. (2020). Lottery-related anomalies: The role of reference-dependent preferences. *Management Science, 66*(1), 473–501.

Baek, S., & Lee, K. Y. (2021). The risk transmission of COVID-19 in the US stock market. *Applied Economics, 53*(17), 1976–1990.

Barber, B. M., & Odean, T. (2000). Trading is hazardous to your wealth: The common stock investment performance of individual investors. *The Journal of Finance, 55*(2), 773–806.

Barberis, N., & Thaler, R. (2003). A survey of behavioral finance. In G. M. Constantinides, M. Harris, & R. M. Stulz (Eds.), *Handbook of the economics of finance* (Vol. 1, pp. 1053–1128). Elsevier.

Ben-David, I., Graham, J. R., & Harvey, C. R. (2013). Managerial miscalibration. *The Quarterly Journal of Economics, 128*(4), 1547–1584.

Bikhchandani, S., Hirshleifer, D., & Welch, I. (1992). A theory of fads, fashion, custom, and cultural change as informational cascades. *Journal of Political Economy, 100*(5), 992–1026.

Boutros, M., Ben-David, I., Graham, J. R., Harvey, C. R., & Payne, J. W. (2020). *The persistence of miscalibration*. National Bureau of Economic Research.

DellaVigna, S., & Pollet, J. M. (2009). Investor inattention and Friday earnings announcements. *The Journal of Finance, 64*(2), 709–749.

Glaser, M., & Weber, M. (2007). Overconfidence and trading volume: Evidence from market experiments. *Journal of Financial Markets, 10*(2), 100–130.

Hirshleifer, D., & Shumway, T. (2003). Good day sunshine: Stock returns and the weather. *The Journal of Finance, 58*(3), 1009–1032.

Kahneman, D., & Tversky, A. (1979). Prospect theory: An analysis of decision under risk. *Econometrica, 47*(2), 263–292.

Raimundo Júnior, G. D. S., Palazzi, R. B., Tavares, R. D. S., & Klotzle, M. C. (2022). Market stress and herding: A new approach to the cryptocurrency market. *Journal of Behavioral Finance, 23*(1), 43–57.

Shiller, R. J. (2000). *Irrational exuberance*. Princeton University Press.

Thaler, R. H., & Sunstein, C. R. (2008). *Nudge: Improving decisions about health, wealth, and happiness*. Penguin Books.

Chapter 8
Market Inefficiencies and Behavioural Influences

Market inefficiencies are the market's method of disclosing its secrets, showing flaws in what is often assumed to be a flawless, logical system. While conventional finance has long claimed that prices represent all available information, behavioural finance contends that the market is a stage in which human psychology plays an outsized role, distorting pricing and causing anomalies that defy rationality (Vasileiou, 2022). These inefficiencies—whether the irrational frenzy of IPOs, the predictable cycles of the January effect, or the speculative hysteria around cryptocurrencies—provide glimpses into our collective mentality, moulded as much by fear, optimism, and overconfidence as by statistics and earnings reports.

In this chapter, we delve into the intriguing area of market inefficiencies, looking at how investor behaviour drives price fluctuations that seem to violate the fundamentals of rational investment. What causes investors to hold onto losing equities while selling winners too soon? Why does the market occasionally surge on Mondays and then droop on Fridays? As we investigate these oddities, we'll discover the psychological motivations that underpin them, such as fear of missing out, loss aversion, recency bias, and the allure of the crowd. Each inefficiency reflects human nature—an interplay of logic and emotion, resulting in patterns that seasoned investors have learnt to spot and, in some circumstances, benefit from.

8.1 Momentum Investing

Momentum investing is the financial equivalent of surfing a wave when you purchase companies that are already rising with the expectation that they will continue to rise. It's an appealing inefficiency in which investors ignore facts and logic in order to follow what seems to be an unstoppable trend. Imagine standing on the brink of a cresting wave, confident that if you grab it at the perfect time, it will propel you onwards to inconceivable heights (Malmendier & Nagel, 2011). Momentum

K. L. Ooi, *Demystifying Behavioral Finance*,
https://doi.org/10.1007/978-981-96-2690-8_8

investing appeals to a fundamental human desire: to be a part of something significant and to share in the highs of achievement with others. In the appropriate circumstances, it's pretty lucrative. In the wrong circumstances, it may be catastrophic.

Behind momentum investing lies a potent psychological combination of recency bias and herd behaviour. When a stock jumps, investors believe that the recent past is a solid indicator of the future. They presume that simply because a stock has been growing, it will continue to do so. People then engage in herd behaviour, fearing that they will lose out on the subsequent significant gain after seeing others purchase shares. This combination produces a feedback cycle in which investors continue to buy into the rise, driving prices further higher. According to research, momentum investing may provide returns that are 6–10% higher than the market average over short periods, making it appealing as a winning strategy. However, like with all market waves, impetus ultimately fades.

The late 1990s tech boom was a textbook example of unbridled momentum investing. Tech stocks soared, sometimes without a strong base of sales or profit. Between 1995 and 2000, the Nasdaq skyrocketed 400%, fuelled chiefly by momentum as investors sought the 'next Microsoft' or 'next Amazon'. Everyone wanted in, and stocks with no track record or profits were selling at skyrocketing prices. However, when the bubble burst in early 2000, many momentum-driven equities collapsed, leaving investors with enormous losses. The wave they'd been riding transformed into a violent undertow, pulling them down.

Momentum investment is widespread in high-growth, high-excitement industries such as technology, biotech, and cryptocurrencies, where innovation inspires optimism and price gains seem inevitable. For example, in the early days of Bitcoin's growth, investors purchased it not for its usefulness but because they watched others become wealthy and dreaded losing out. Bitcoin skyrocketed from roughly $1000 to over $20,000 in under a year, but the velocity proved unsustainable. By early 2018, Bitcoin's value had fallen below $7000, demonstrating how risky it can be to pursue momentum without recognising the underlying issues.

Momentum investing is appealing—and dangerous—because of its short-term attractiveness. According to Jegadeesh and Titman's research, equities that perform well during a 3- to 12-month period generally maintain that trend in the short term but often underperform in the long run. Momentum is an appealing approach for investors looking to earn rapid profits, but it may change at any time. The fundamental danger of momentum investing is that it relies on communal excitement, and when that enthusiasm fades, those who still own the stock are left high and dry.

Finally, momentum investing is more about psychology than money. It's the excitement of the chase, the appeal of being on the winning squad, and the dread of losing out. However, like any emotion-driven tactic, momentum should be approached with prudence. Momentum may offer spectacular profits, but it can also result in painful losses for those who ride the wave too long, forgetting that every trend ultimately slows and falls.

8.2 The Small-Firm Effect

The small company effect is an unusual market inefficiency that challenges the dominance of large-cap stocks by implying that small-cap businesses—those with smaller market capitalisations—outperform their more prominent rivals over time. It is this inefficiency that encourages investors to go beyond the significant names to find 'hidden gems' with the potential for explosive development. From tiny regional banks to specialist technology enterprises, these organisations often slip under the radar, resulting in undervaluation and potential. Historical evidence confirms the small company effect: research going back to the 1980s shows that small-cap equities in the United States beat large-cap stocks by an average of 2–3% every year.

Why has this impact persisted? According to behavioural finance, the small business impact is primarily due to overconfidence bias and anchoring. Investors and analysts often prioritise big, well-known corporations with established reputations, causing them to overlook or undervalue smaller enterprises (Hirshleifer & Shumway, 2003). This 'anchoring' to large-cap equities generates a market gap in which small-cap stocks are either ignored or underestimated. Overconfidence also plays a role since investors believe that more prominent firms are 'safer' owing to their brand familiarity and consistent profitability. This tendency exposes small-cap companies to mispricing, enabling astute investors to take advantage of the market's inefficiency.

The performance of small-cap equities in the aftermath of financial crises demonstrates the small-company effect. Following the 2008 recession, small-cap stocks in the Russell 2000 Index increased by more than 30% in 2010, compared to around 15% for the S&P 500. Investors seeking strong growth during the recovery period went to tiny caps, driving them upward. This rally proved the strength of the small business impact, as these 'underdogs' outperformed market leaders during moments of economic recovery. A similar tendency has been seen internationally, with small businesses outperforming more giant corporations during times of economic boom.

However, small business impact comes with hazards. Small-cap stocks are more volatile, with smaller trading volumes and greater susceptibility to market circumstances. In a downturn, they may suffer disproportionately since their meagre resources leave them susceptible to economic shocks. Given the volatility, investors must have a higher risk tolerance and a longer investing horizon. However, for those who can weather the storm, the opportunity for profit is substantial since tiny businesses often outperform their bigger rivals.

8.3 Value vs. Growth Anomaly

The value versus the growth paradox challenges the widely held belief that high-growth equities should constantly beat those of stable, cheap firms. While growth companies entice investors with the promise of quick growth, historical evidence shows that 'value' stocks—those with low price-to-earnings or price-to-book ratios—outperform in the long run. This anomaly tests investor assumptions and highlights the risks of following the present trend. Over the previous century, value stocks in the United States have generated 10.7% average annual returns, compared to 9.6% for growth companies, demonstrating that slow and steady may win the race (Glaser & Weber, 2007).

Optimism bias is a significant psychological element behind this oddity. Investors often forecast aggressive growth rates for high-profile firms, focussing on prospective rather than existing profitability. Tech behemoths such as Tesla and Amazon, for example, have captured the market's imagination with promises of game-changing innovation. However, this euphoria may drive values to unsustainable heights, leaving growth companies exposed to sharp declines. Meanwhile, value stocks—unremarkable but financially sound—are often disregarded despite providing consistent returns and financial stability.

The tech boom of the 1990s and early 2000s vividly exemplified this phenomenon. Investors, fuelled by optimism bias, poured money into Internet-based growth firms, driving their values to unprecedented heights. When the bubble broke, these expensive growth companies fell, but conventional value equities, such as those in the utilities or consumer staples sectors, remained stable. During this time, value investors who were patient with their portfolios outperformed others who pursued high-growth tales that eventually fizzled out.

Confirmation bias exaggerates the value vs. growth anomaly. Investors who are enthusiastic about growth companies often seek information that confirms their expectations, disregarding red flags or rejecting vital news as irrelevant. When a high-growth company does well, investors tend to double down. They ignore value stocks, considering them 'boring' and unworthy of attention. This generates a cycle in which growth companies are bought up, and value equities become undervalued, presenting possible bargains for conscientious investors.

For those with a long-term view, the value vs. growth anomaly reminds them to prioritise fundamentals above hype. While growth stocks may provide remarkable short-term gains, they are generally associated with more volatility and risk. Value stocks, with their solid profits and lower valuations, serve as a counterweight to market speculation, providing consistent long-term gains. This oddity emphasises the ancient knowledge that often the finest chances are not in the showy, high-growth industries but in the humble, trustworthy enterprises that are the backbone of the economy.

8.4 The Weekend Effect

The weekend effect is a puzzling market oddity in which equities perform worse on Mondays than on other weekdays, calling into question the concept of consistent, reasonable pricing. This tendency has been noticed for decades and is visible in a variety of markets. According to research, average Monday returns are 0.25% lower than those on other weekdays (Boutros et al., 2020). It's as if the market, like many of us, begins the week with Monday blues. Despite several explanations, this inefficiency is mainly unexplained, making it one of the most attractive financial anomalies.

One possibility is that the investor's attitude and mood shifted over the weekend. During this period, investors are away from the daily trading rush and tend to become more introspective, which leads to heightened anxiety and risk aversion. By Monday, this increased prudence has translated into selling pressure, as investors choose to exit holdings rather than take on new risks. Behavioural finance research suggests that emotions play a more significant role in trading than many people realise, with Monday's pessimism pushing prices down in a self-reinforcing loop.

Data show that the weekend impact persists. In a survey of US markets, French (1980) discovered consistently lower returns on Mondays, a tendency replicated in foreign markets ranging from Tokyo to London. Even with advanced trading algorithms, the Monday slump continues despite efforts to neutralise it. Some hedge funds and institutions consciously avoid heavy trading on Mondays, recognising that poor liquidity exacerbates this pattern. Their actions, however, add to the impact since lower institutional purchasing exacerbates the downward pressure.

Institutional behaviour also significantly influences the market. Many significant funds and asset managers plan important trading decisions for later in the week, avoiding Mondays owing to the expected poor market mood. This 'wait and see' attitude reduces demand on Mondays, strengthening the trend for prices to fall. Individual traders and day traders might take advantage of this inefficiency by anticipating weekly trends and entering at the predicted Monday dip.

In the larger scheme of things, the weekend impact may seem insignificant, but it highlights the broader notion that markets are not entirely logical. Emotion and Calendar Effect influence price changes. For investors prepared to go beyond figures and measurements, the weekend effect illustrates that the market's inefficiencies may be driven by very human characteristics, making even the cold world of finance more approachable.

8.5 Neglect of Long-Term Fundamentals in High-Volatility Stocks

High-volatility stocks regularly make headlines, garnering attention with fast price fluctuations that promise quick returns but usually deviate from their genuine worth. Prices in many circumstances vary dramatically, driven more by speculation and short-term enthusiasm than by long-term fundamentals. This disregard for long-term fundamentals is an example of market inefficiency, in which investors prioritise short-term price movement above financial stability, profitability, and sustainable development. The appeal is strong: who wouldn't be lured to a stock that has quadrupled overnight? However, this obsession with volatility often leads to inflated prices and eventual collapses.

This inefficiency is driven by attention bias and overconfidence. High-volatility equities, which are commonly found in areas such as biotech, technology, or developing markets, attract attention because they are newsworthy. Headlines about a breakthrough medication or creative technology pique investors' interest, causing them to assume that these companies are on the verge of greatness. Overconfidence exacerbates the problem, as investors believe they are on the verge of discovering the next great thing (Baker & Ricciardi, 2014). However, the reality is typically more humdrum since the corporations that own these stocks usually need more profits or stability to support their absurd values.

During the biotech bubble of the early 2010s, for example, minor biotech companies saw their stock values skyrocket when promising medications were announced. Investors flocked to these companies, enticed by compelling tales and a quest for huge profits, sending prices higher. However, when the FDA rejected some treatments or clinical studies failed, these companies fell precipitously, leaving investors who had overlooked fundamentals with significant losses. The volatility was exhilarating, but those who had bought into the hype were often disappointed.

The Bitcoin market is another example. Bitcoin and other digital assets have sparked worldwide interest with their quick price fluctuations and tales of overnight billionaires. However, many investors acquire cryptocurrencies not for their intrinsic worth but because they view volatility as an opportunity. Bitcoin skyrocketed from roughly $30,000 to $64,000 in only a few months in 2021, only to plummet again, owing partly to speculative trading and media hype. Investors who bought in based on headlines were left at the mercy of a turbulent market, disconnected from the long-term fundamentals that often stabilise more conventional assets.

The beauty of market inefficiencies is that they provide insight into how we, as investors, often behave against our own best interests. These inefficiencies are more than simply anomalies to be fixed; they are reminders of the power of psychology on market results, reflecting the human impulses that make investing such an exciting and sometimes humbling endeavour (An et al., 2020). When investors follow trends, neglect fundamentals, or trade on rumours, they create the perfect environment for inefficiencies—price fluctuations that defy logic but seem all too natural at the moment.

Understanding these inefficiencies provides us with more than just market intelligence; it also gives us insight into ourselves. Each inefficiency demonstrates how biases such as overconfidence, herd behaviour, and loss aversion influence our judgements, frequently closing our eyes to the broader picture. Recognising these patterns teaches us to examine our instincts, pulling back from the emotional undertow that has driven many investors to chase highs and avoid losses at all costs. Behavioural finance not only identifies where markets deviate from logic, but it also teaches us how to negotiate these deviations critically.

References

An, L., Wang, H., Wang, J., & Yu, J. (2020). Lottery-related anomalies: The role of reference-dependent preferences. *Management Science, 66*(1), 473–501.

Baker, H. K., & Ricciardi, V. (2014). Behavioral aspects of financial planning and investing. *Management Research Review, 37*(10), 818–828.

Boutros, M., Ben-David, I., Graham, J. R., Harvey, C. R., & Payne, J. W. (2020). *The persistence of miscalibration (No. w28010)*. National Bureau of Economic Research.

Glaser, M., & Weber, M. (2007). Overconfidence and trading volume. *The Geneva Risk and Insurance Review, 32*, 1–36.

Hirshleifer, D., & Shumway, T. (2003). Good day sunshine: Stock returns and the weather. *The Journal of Finance, 58*(3), 1009–1032.

Malmendier, U., & Nagel, S. (2011). Depression babies: Do macroeconomic experiences affect risk-taking? *The Quarterly Journal of Economics, 126*(1), 373–416.

Vasileiou, E. (2022). Behavioral finance and algorithmic trading: Understanding psychological impacts. *Behavioral Finance Review*.

Part III
The Future of Behavioural Finance

The future of behavioural finance promotes research into the evolution of this dynamic field and its growing importance in a society marked by rapid technological advancements, shifting global economies, and increasingly complex financial structures. Although behavioural finance has altered our understanding of markets and decision-making, its future is even more promising. This section looks at how growing technology, social shifts, and a better knowledge of human behaviour are reshaping the financial landscape and creating unprecedented opportunities for investors, lawmakers, and scholars.

The rise of artificial intelligence, machine learning, and big data analytics will have a significant impact on the future of behavioural finance. These technologies are revolutionising market processes, as well as human behaviour analysis and prediction. Consider systems capable of analysing millions of transactions in real time, identifying patterns of overconfidence or herd behaviour as they emerge. AI allows us to go beyond passive observation of behavioural biases and actively minimise them, supporting investors in making more logical and less emotionally impacted decisions. As robots improve their understanding of human conduct, they also acquire our flaws. Algorithmic trading algorithms, although apparently rational, may accentuate biases inherent in their training data, causing further problems for market stability.

This section investigates the role of behavioural finance in addressing major global concerns of our day. As environmental, social, and governance (ESG) problems gain importance, it is critical to understand investor views and reactions to ESG features. Behavioural insights explain why some investors choose sustainable assets while others are sceptical. Behavioural finance explains the psychological motives underlying these decisions, allowing the alignment of values with actions and allocating resources to initiatives that benefit long-term societal goals. The Bitcoin revolution offers a new area in which behavioural finance will be critical. The cryptocurrency market, which is defined by high volatility, speculative exuberance, and the lack of traditional valuation methods, serves as a real-time laboratory for studying investor psychology. Behavioural finance will be critical in understanding the emotional aspects that influence Bitcoin adoption, such as fear of missing out and the attractiveness of decentralisation. As digital assets gain traction, these results will inform investment strategies and regulatory regimes aimed at protecting investors while encouraging innovation.

Furthermore, the future of behavioural finance extends beyond markets to include the whole financial ecosystem. As financial literacy programmes spread over the globe, behavioural principles may improve their effectiveness by addressing the cognitive and emotional barriers that prevent individuals from making sound financial decisions. Consider instructional programmes that teach not just the basics of saving and investing but also how to detect and overcome biases like loss aversion and present bias. We can create a more inclusive financial system by training individuals with behavioural skills, allowing them to achieve their goals more successfully.

This section investigates the ethical implications of behavioural finance as it increasingly intersects with technology and politics. Companies and governments gain a deeper knowledge of human behaviour, giving them the ability to influence decisions—sometimes for the better, sometimes for the worst. Behavioural nudges, although often meant to promote positive outcomes, may also be used to regulate client conduct. The future of behavioural finance must address these ethical problems by ensuring that its applications prioritise justice, transparency, and social well-being.

Finally, the future of behavioural finance portrays a field at the crossroads of innovation and contemplation. It is a future in which behavioural insights extend beyond academia and actively affect market interactions, policy design, and financial education techniques. AI-driven technologies that diminish emotional decision-making, as well as strategies that relate investment to global environmental goals, provide endless prospects.

After finishing this section, you will perceive behavioural finance not just as a tool for understanding the past or managing the present but also as a paradigm for shaping the future. Behavioural finance offers an interesting viewpoint for investors adjusting to the changing financial environment, regulators dealing with systemic issues, and academics pushing the boundaries of knowledge. The future remains unpredictable, but using behavioural finance as a framework, we may navigate its complexities with more clarity and purpose. Welcome to the next stage in the evolution of behavioural finance—a stage in which human behaviour, technology, and global innovation converge to revolutionise the basic structure of markets and economies.

Chapter 9
Emerging Trends and AI Technologies

In the financial world, change is the only constant, and today's market is moving quicker than ever. Artificial intelligence and new technologies are more than simply tools; they are game-changers, altering the investment and financial environment in previously imagined ways. AI is creating a new bar for speed, precision, and intelligence, with robo-advisors providing personalised portfolios and predictive algorithms forecasting market movements with astounding accuracy. These innovations aren't simply improving old tactics; they're ushering in a future in which data-driven intelligence and automation lead the way, making the market more accessible and responsive to all investors, large and small.

This chapter delves into five transformative themes in finance: AI-driven sentiment analysis, high-frequency trading, robo-advisors, blockchain and decentralised finance, and natural language processing. Each of these advancements introduces new capabilities, as well as new questions. How can AI determine investor sentiment from social media chatter? What implications does the emergence of decentralised finance have for conventional banks? These developments point to a future in which investors can make better choices quicker, and data becomes more than just statistics on a screen; it becomes an active blueprint for profit and success. As we investigate these examples, we discover a financial environment dominated by algorithms, automation, and access, providing a look into the future of money itself.

9.1 AI-Driven Sentiment Analysis: Decoding the Market's Emotional Pulse

Imagine being able to tap into the emotions of millions of investors at the same time, understanding the collective mood that drives each decision and market fluctuation. AI-powered sentiment analysis is making this a reality by converting massive quantities of Internet discussion, news articles, and social media postings into actionable

K. L. Ooi, *Demystifying Behavioral Finance*,
https://doi.org/10.1007/978-981-96-2690-8_9

insights. It's a powerful instrument that reveals investor psychology, enabling financial institutions to understand the tiny fluctuations in mood that may cause significant price swings. Far beyond just watching figures on a screen, AI sentiment analysis delves into the core of market behaviour, converting raw emotions into quantitative facts (Ackert & Deaves, 2009).

One example is BlackRock's Aladdin platform, which has become a standard for institutional investors. Aladdin scours billions of data points—headlines, tweets, and opinions—every second, judging the tone, frequency, and substance of talks about specific stocks or sectors. During times of market uncertainty, such as the early phases of the COVID-19 epidemic, Aladdin and other technologies revealed insights that conventional data could not. Aladdin was able to identify surges in concern about specific sectors, enabling BlackRock to reallocate resources ahead of swings in investor sentiment, providing them an advantage during one of the most turbulent periods in recent history (Boutros et al., 2020).

However, AI sentiment analysis benefits more than simply institutional investors. Platforms like MarketPsych have made this technology available to regular investors, democratising insights that were previously restricted to Wall Street giants. MarketPsych's algorithms, for example, gather social media sentiment and differentiate between optimism and pessimism for specific stocks or sectors. Individual investors who tap into this stream of emotional input receive insight into market movements before they fully materialise, allowing them to act rather than react.

However, the growth of AI sentiment analysis raises ethical concerns. Can computers capture human emotion in a manner that accurately represents market mood, or do they risk increasing noise over substance? There is a risk that sentiment monitoring may lead investors to act on transient sentiments, aggravating market volatility. Furthermore, in a world where false news and disinformation spread like wildfire, sentiment analysis algorithms may fail to distinguish between genuine investor sentiment and fabricated hype. A poorly configured model might readily misread data, perhaps leading to mistaken trades based on incorrect indications.

Looking forward, the next generation of sentiment analysis will most certainly include even more precise natural language processing (NLP) algorithms capable of detecting tone subtleties as well as disinformation. Soon, these algorithms may be able to discern between real investor insights and mere market rumours, hence improving forecast accuracy. This progress has the potential to make AI-driven sentiment analysis one of the most powerful tools in finance, allowing us to comprehend not just investor sentiment but also the emotions that impact the market. The ability to traverse these emotional currents may be the difference between capitalising on a trend and falling prey to market sentiment fluctuations.

9.2 AI's Precision in Stock Selection: Data, Patterns, and Predictive Power

AI has a disruptive impact on stock selection and investment, fundamentally changing the operation of financial markets. Using AI's outstanding capacity to analyse on large datasets, investors may gain significant insights and efficiency. However, AI's transformative potential introduces disruptive forces, amplifying risks, ethical quandaries, and structural flaws. A thorough assessment of AI's function reveals two characteristics: a powerful tool for precision and an unforeseen disruptor.

AI has emerged as a breakthrough tool in stock selection, enabling unparalleled accuracy in identifying investing opportunities via data analysis, pattern recognition, and predictive insight production. In an era where financial markets generate an enormous amount of data every day, AI's ability to comprehend, synthesise, and react to diverse datasets provides a huge edge. This precision not only helps decision-making, but it also changes the way investors see and grasp market complexities.

The core of AI's accuracy is its ability to handle data at a scale and pace that human analysts cannot comprehend. Conventional stock selection is based on systematic financial metrics such as price-to-earnings ratios, earnings growth, and dividend yield. Although somewhat useful, these metrics often overlook the complex dynamics of modern markets. AI overcomes these limits by combining unstructured data sources such as news stories, social media material, satellite imagery, and macroeconomic indicators. AI can analyse real-time geopolitical developments with firm earnings reports to forecast sector-wide repercussions. This multilayered study allows investors to forecast market changes with more accuracy than traditional methods.

The ability of AI to detect hidden patterns and correlations in large datasets is an important application. Machine learning algorithms have been employed to investigate weather patterns and their impacts on agricultural commodities, providing useful information for agribusiness stock investments. AI has been used to estimate business performance by analysing parking lot occupancy using satellite imagery. By combining these atypical data sources with normal financial indicators, AI creates a holistic view of a company's future, delivering previously unreachable insights.

AI's predictive potential is particularly evident in sentiment analysis, a subset of natural language processing. Sentiment analysis evaluates the tone and content of textual data to determine market sentiment. For example, AI can scan a large number of news articles, social media posts, and earnings conference transcripts to determine investor sentiment towards a certain stock or sector. Positive sentiment may signal an upward trend, while negative sentiment may anticipate a decline. By quantifying these patterns, AI provides investors with quick indications of market mood, allowing for timely and strategic response.

Furthermore, AI exhibits expertise in adapting to changing market conditions via dynamic modelling. Traditional stock selection approaches rely on established criteria and historical averages, making them less effective in volatile or unpredictable markets. Nonetheless, AI continues to progress by integrating more information. During economic downturns, AI may shift its focus to defensive equities in sectors like utilities or healthcare. In contrast, during a bull market, it may favour high-growth shares in the technology or consumer discretionary sectors. This adaptability ensures that investment approaches remain relevant even in rapidly changing environments.

An example of AI's accuracy is its role in thematic investing. Investors are increasingly looking to align their portfolios with long-term global trends such as renewable energy, technological innovation, and ESG (environmental, social, and governance) factors. This process is improved by artificial intelligence, which examines diverse datasets to discover organisations that are strategically positioned to benefit on these themes. AI can find high-potential stocks in the renewable energy business by analysing government legislation, technological breakthroughs, and corporate plans. This expertise not only increases earnings, but it also connects investments to broader societal goals.

Although AI has transformative potential, its predictive powers are laden with issues. One notable problem is its reliance on past data, which may not accurately capture the complexities of rare events. During the COVID-19 pandemic, AI models built on pre-pandemic data struggled to react to the fast changes in consumer behaviour, supply chain disruptions, and government measures. This restriction emphasises the necessity for human supervision to contextualise AI-generated insights, ensuring their usefulness in unexpected contexts. Another problem is the danger of overfitting, which occurs when AI models become too tailored to past data, misclassifying outliers as trends. This may lead to inaccurate estimates and poor investment decisions. Nonetheless, as AI technology advances, improvements in machine learning algorithms reduce these obstacles, making projections more robust and reliable.

9.3 AI's Role in Behavioural Biases

Behavioural biases, which are deeply embedded in human psychology, have been identified as significant factors to irrational decision-making in financial markets. Cognitive biases including overconfidence, herd behaviour, loss aversion, and confirmation bias may lead investors to act against their best interests. Artificial intelligence (AI), due to its impartial and data-driven traits, has become an excellent tool for mitigating biases, offering a rational counterweight to the unpredictability of human behaviour in investment decisions.

The heart of AI's ability to mitigate behavioural biases is its reliance on objective data and logical processing. AI algorithms, unlike human investors, examine information objectively, focussing exclusively on patterns, trends, and probabilities. During market volatility, when worry causes many investors to panic and sell or conserve funds, AI systems retain their cool, determining if market movements signal intrinsic problems or temporary disruptions. This detachment from emotional decision-making allows AI to deliver clarity and stability in unpredictable circumstances.

An example of this is the reduction of overconfidence bias, a common mistake among investors who overestimate their ability to foresee market changes or outperform benchmarks. Overconfidence often leads to overtrading, inaccurate risk assessments, and inadequate portfolio diversification. AI mitigates this by drawing decisions based on objective facts rather than subjective preconceptions. Machine learning algorithms may examine historical performance and current market conditions to recommend optimal trading strategies, therefore reducing impulsive decisions powered by overconfidence. Furthermore, AI's ability to continuously learn and adapt ensures that strategies evolve in response to changing conditions, reducing the impact of overconfidence on investment outcomes.

Similarly, AI reduces herd behaviour, a cognitive bias in which investors adhere to the majority, frequently resulting in speculative booms or unexpected market crashes. Herd behaviour is clearly seen in events such as the dot-com bubble and the present meme stock craze, in which communal euphoria or fear accelerates prices well beyond their intrinsic merits. AI's analytical accuracy enables it to quickly discover deviations from fundamentals, revealing overvalued assets or suggesting opportunities in low-cost enterprises that the majority ignores. During the GameStop and AMC crazes, retail investors aggravated the issue, while AI-powered systems highlighted the unsustainable nature of these price changes, providing an important logical perspective.

Loss aversion, a frequent cognitive bias, causes investors to prioritise avoiding losses above achieving equivalent returns, resulting in overly cautious strategies or irrational sell-offs during market dips. This inclination may be dangerous, particularly in volatile markets where short-term losses may obscure long-term possibilities. AI, which is immune to emotional reactions, evaluates the risk-reward profile of assets objectively. During a market downturn, AI systems may suggest holding or purchasing low-cost assets based on their long-term potential rather than succumbing to the fear-induced urge to sell. By prioritising facts over emotion, AI helps investors maintain discipline and adopt strategies that align with their financial goals.

AI also reduces confirmation bias, which is the tendency to seek information that supports prior beliefs while ignoring opposing evidence. Investors often fall victim to this trap, selectively selecting evidence that supports their market view or investment judgements. AI assesses all relevant information objectively, ensuring that conclusions are based on rigorous study rather than selective interpretation. For example, when evaluating a firm, AI systems may include financial reports, industry trends, macroeconomic statistics, and sentiment analysis, offering a holistic perspective that challenges preconceptions and encourages informed decision-making.

In addition to reducing individual biases, AI improves market stability by calming the collective emotional oscillations that often characterise financial markets. AI acts as a stabilising force by making consistent and reasonable recommendations in a variety of situations, hence lowering the degree of market overreaction. This is particularly important at times of crisis, such as the 2008 financial crash or the COVID-19 pandemic, when investor behaviour is characterised by fear and uncertainty. In these cases, AI systems increase liquidity and trust by discovering discounted opportunities and providing actionable insights that prevent panic-induced sell-offs.

Nonetheless, utilising AI to combat behavioural biases poses certain challenges. A major risk is overreliance on AI systems, which allows investors to totally rely on algorithms without understanding their limitations. Although AI is excellent at data processing, it is not perfect and may misinterpret signals or ignore uncommon events. Several AI models struggled to adapt to quick economic shifts and diverse market dynamics during the COVID-19 outbreak, emphasising the need of human supervision in contextualising AI-generated insights.

Another concern is that AI may unintentionally intensify biases rather than relieving them. AI systems trained on biased past data may perpetuate present market inefficiencies. For example, if a model prioritises short-term profitability above long-term stability, it may encourage speculative trading, hence increasing volatility. To prevent these dangers, AI systems must be built with strong checks and balances that ensure alignment with investors' long-term interests and ethical standards.

Although AI offers many benefits, its widespread use raises significant risks and potential disruptions to financial systems. Many AI systems are inherently opaque, which is a serious concern. These algorithms, particularly those that use deep learning, often create predictions or conclusions without providing explicit explanations. This lack of transparency creates challenges for both investors and regulators. How can investors trust the rationale behind an AI system's stock recommendation if the underlying logic is opaque? This opacity may lead to an undue reliance on AI, jeopardising the accountability and monitoring required for successful decision-making.

Furthermore, the quickness and effectiveness of AI may increase market volatility. High-frequency trading (HFT) systems, powered by artificial intelligence, execute deals in milliseconds, often responding to minor market fluctuations or abnormalities. This may increase liquidity, but it also increases the risk of flash crashes, which are sudden and substantial price decreases caused by automated trading systems reacting simultaneously to market events. The infamous 'Flash Crash' of 2010, in which the Dow Jones Industrial Average dropped over 1000 points in minutes, shows algorithmic trading's ability to destabilise markets.

Another disruptive feature of AI is its ability to increase systemic weaknesses. Many AI models are trained on historical data, making them inherently retrospective. When unusual occurrences, such as the COVID-19 pandemic, disrupt markets, AI systems may struggle to adapt, resulting in repeated failures. Several AI-driven investment models struggled to adjust to the quick global consequences of lockdowns, supply chain disruptions, and shifting consumer behaviours during the pandemic's early stages. This restriction emphasises the need of human supervision and adaptability in the management of AI systems.

As artificial intelligence grows more prevalent, ethical and regulatory challenges become more important. A major concern is the concentration of AI's benefits within a small group of institutional investors and technologically advanced enterprises. Advanced AI systems need significant resources—access to private data, computing power, and specialist expertise—which are often unavailable to ordinary investors. This disparity threatens to create a divided market in which institutional actors dominate while regular investors struggle to compete.

Regulators have the difficult problem of ensuring that AI-powered systems operate fairly and transparently. What safeguards can be put in place to prevent AI from being used to manipulate markets or exploit vulnerabilities? Predatory algorithms, for example, may utilise spoofing (submitting fake orders to manipulate prices) or exploit inefficiencies in less liquid markets. Achieving a balance between supporting innovation and maintaining market integrity will be a big task in the coming years.

AI represents both a shift and a rethink of stock picking and investment. Its ability to assess large datasets, adapt to changing conditions, and remove human biases is unparalleled. It democratises access to smart technology, allowing investors to make better decisions and navigate increasingly complex markets. However, its limitations—insufficient transparency, danger of systemic disruption, and ethical quandaries—highlight the need for caution.

Our answer to these challenges will determine the future of AI in investment. Hybrid models, which combine AI's computational skills with human judgement, may give the best answer. Using AI for data-intensive operations, along with human intuition and oversight for strategic decisions, allows investors to decrease risks while increasing opportunities. Finally, artificial intelligence is neither innately good nor bad; it is just a tool. The impact on stock selection and investment is determined by how it is used, who uses it, and the restrictions put in place to prevent abuse. As we go forward, the question is not whether AI will revolutionise markets—it has already done so—but how we can best exploit its potential, ensuring equal distribution of its benefits while limiting related risks.

9.4 High-Frequency Trading: The Microsecond Race that's Reshaping Markets

Success in the hyper-competitive world of high-frequency trading (HFT) is evaluated in microseconds, not seconds or milliseconds. HFT businesses such as Virtu Financial and Citadel Securities have used speed as their ultimate weapon, completing thousands of deals in the blink of an eye to catch minuscule price variations that human traders would miss. In a world where the smallest distance between two locations may be worth millions, HFT corporations have constructed a financial empire on the basis of split-second choices. They are more than simply market players; they are the hidden forces that drive liquidity and, at times, volatility.

High-frequency trading presently accounts for more than half of all equities trading activity in the United States, fundamentally changing the stock market's dynamics. HFT businesses capitalise on inefficiencies that typical traders would never see by using complicated algorithms that scan data, recognise patterns, and execute trades nearly immediately. These algorithms are so precisely calibrated that even a few microseconds—the time it takes for data to travel down a fibreoptic cable—can put a business at a disadvantage. To remain competitive, HFT businesses spend extensively on proximity to stock exchanges and cutting-edge microwave equipment, shaving off critical microseconds to preserve their advantage.

However, the growth of HFT has provoked widespread discussion over its influence on market stability. The 2010 Flash Crash remains a frightening example: the Dow Jones Industrial Average fell over 1000 points in minutes before recovering, owing partly to algorithmic trading that amplified sell-offs (Hirshleifer, 2015). Critics claim that, although HFT offers liquidity, it also generates tremendous volatility, causing markets to endure unexpected, dramatic collapses. In these high-speed conditions, the same algorithms meant to profit from modest price swings may increase market stress, posing systemic hazards.

Global regulators are becoming more concerned about the effects of HFT. They've started investigating techniques to restrict trading speed or volume to prevent flash crashes and keep the market stable. For example, the European Union adopted the Markets in Financial Instruments Directive II (MiFID II), which requires HFT businesses to register and follow more onerous restrictions. While these restrictions are a start towards reducing volatility, the financial sector is still split on whether the advantages of HFT, such as enhanced liquidity, exceed the hazards.

As HFT technology progresses, corporations are focussing on AI-driven algorithms that adapt in real time, learning from prior market behaviour to predict trends before they arise. However, this change raises the issue of whether markets will become more efficient or unpredictable. The future of HFT will likely include a balancing act in which speed and complexity must be balanced with appropriate trading methods. Finally, high-frequency trading is altering what it means to compete in financial markets, providing a look into a future in which speed and technology rule supreme—but not without consequence.

9.5 Robo-Advisors: Revolutionising Wealth Management for the Masses

The emergence of robo-advisors has caused a seismic upheaval in the world of wealth management. Platforms such as Betterment, Wealthfront, and Schwab Intelligent Portfolios use AI to provide individualised investing solutions to everyone, from experienced investors to newbies who may be frightened by conventional financial advice. Robo-advisers have upended the world of financial planning by providing personalised portfolios and financial advice for a fraction of the cost of human advisors (Ben-David et al., 2013). Customised, data-driven investing advice, formerly reserved for the rich, is now available to the general public.

As of 2023, robo-advisors handle more than $1 trillion in assets worldwide, demonstrating the rising confidence and demand for these AI-powered platforms. The attraction stems from its simplicity and cost. With robo-advisors, investors may answer a few questions about their risk tolerance, financial objectives, and time horizon, and an algorithm will create a personalised portfolio in minutes. These portfolios are then maintained and rebalanced automatically, enabling investors to relax while their assets are handled precisely and consistently. Millennials, in particular, have gravitated to these sites, enticed by the cheap costs and technologically advanced approach that complements their digital lives.

However, robo-advisors are becoming intelligent financial partners rather than just automated investing platforms. Modern robo-advisors include features such as tax loss harvesting and ESG (environmental, social, and governance) screening, enabling users to invest in line with their ideals. Some are even integrating predictive analytics, which uses artificial intelligence to evaluate market situations and change portfolios proactively. This movement mirrors a broader trend in banking, in which technology not only improves but also redefines old services, establishing new standards for efficiency and accessibility.

However, the fast expansion of robo-advisors presents significant problems. Can computers really replace the nuanced, sympathetic guidance given by human advisers, particularly during market downturns when emotions are high? While robo-advisers excel at data-driven judgements, they lack the emotional intelligence that human advisors provide—a feature that is especially important during turbulent times. As these platforms expand, several businesses are experimenting with hybrid models in which robo-advisers handle the majority of portfolio management. Still, consumers may also contact human advisors for more complicated, personalised queries.

The robo-advisor movement is not a fleeting fad; it is a revolution in financial management. As AI technology progresses, robo-advisers will undoubtedly get more polished, combining deeper insights and providing services that conventional advisors may need help to match at comparable prices. In the following years, robo-advisors have the potential to transform financial planning by making investment accessible, inexpensive, and personalised for millions of consumers who would otherwise be excluded from the wealth management industry.

9.6 Blockchain and Decentralised Finance (DeFi): Finance Without Borders

Blockchain technology and decentralised finance, or DeFi, are ushering in a new age in which financial transactions are conducted directly between individuals, with no banks or intermediaries involved. DeFi, which uses blockchain's transparent, secure, and irreversible record, enables users to lend, borrow, and exchange assets without the need for a central authority. This revolution is more than simply technical; it is conceptual, undermining centuries-old financial institutions and providing consumers with unprecedented authority over their assets. The entire value of DeFi protocols topped $100 billion in 2021, up from less than $1 billion in 2019, demonstrating the industry's tremendous development and potential.

Compound is one of the most widely used DeFi protocols, enabling users to lend and borrow digital assets while receiving variable interest. Unlike conventional banks, where the institution sets rates, Compound's rates are dynamic and driven by real-time supply and demand on the blockchain. This change democratises finance by enabling people from anywhere in the globe to access services that were previously limited by location, banking access, or credit history (Baek & Lee, 2021). Furthermore, since blockchain transactions are validated, customers benefit from transparency, which is sometimes absent in conventional finance, where fees, interest rates, and conditions are opaque.

However, DeFi's fast growth poses new challenges. Security issues are a crucial problem since intelligent contracts, although intended to be safe, are prone to hackers and attacks. In August 2021, the DeFi platform Poly Network was hacked, resulting in a temporary loss of over $600 million in customer assets, the majority of which were eventually recovered. These occurrences highlight the reality that, although innovative, DeFi is still in its early stages, with security mechanisms and user safeguards falling behind conventional banking. Furthermore, regulatory ambiguity hangs around DeFi as governments and financial authorities need help with how to monitor or control transactions that do not involve central banks or financial institutions.

DeFi's success will depend on achieving a balance between decentralisation and security. As more individuals use DeFi, there will be a greater desire for improved safety, either via regulated DeFi platforms or guaranteed intelligent contracts. Blockchain and DeFi are transforming finance by providing an alternative to conventional banking that values openness, control, and inclusion. While the technology is still growing, its ability to democratise banking on a global scale is evident, opening the path for a society in which finance really knows no boundaries.

9.7 Natural Language Processing (NLP): Reading Between the Lines of Financial Data

Natural language processing (NLP) is one of AI's most intriguing applications in finance, enabling computers to comprehend, analyse, and extract meaning from human language. Financial businesses may use natural language processing (NLP) to filter through massive volumes of textual data—earnings call transcripts, financial reports, and market news—and uncover insights that would otherwise be overlooked. This technology has become a vital tool for financial analysts, allowing them to sift not just what is said but also how it is spoken, identifying variations in attitude, emphasis, and tone that may indicate future corporate performance.

Kensho, a business bought by S&P Global, is at the forefront of NLP technology for finance. Kensho's AI algorithms analyse earnings calls for minor clues that may indicate a company's outlook. For example, a change in management's tone on a quarterly results call, from enthusiastic to cautious, might signal possible issues ahead. Kensho's technology has proved especially valuable during earnings season, offering early warnings or confirmations that might influence stock performance. According to studies, NLP-based analysis may increase investment returns by 3–4% since it detects subtleties that conventional financial analysis misses (Königstorfer & Thalmann, 2020).

However, NLP is not without restrictions. Language is intrinsically complicated, with nuance, irony, and cultural context that robots still fail to understand. A cautiously hopeful comment from a CEO may be viewed differently depending on tone, industry conventions, or even regional linguistic differences. Furthermore, NLP algorithms may suffer from false positives, detecting phrases that seem negative or positive out of context. Despite these limitations, the fast progress of NLP promises to close the gaps, ushering in a future in which machines can read language as thoroughly and sensitively as humans.

Looking forward, the future of NLP in finance is expected to include more personalised insights. Consider a programme that not only identifies sentiment but also anticipates its influence on stock performance based on previous patterns or one that tailors investing suggestions to a client's personal preferences for specific linguistic signals. NLP can transform the way investors analyse financial data by going beyond statistics and understanding the narrative behind them. As NLP technology progresses, it may become a standard in economic research, offering investors an advantage by allowing them to 'read between the lines' and unearth insights that data alone cannot convey.

The future of banking is happening in front of us, fuelled by AI's accuracy, speed, and predictive capacity. We are entering a future in which human limitations no longer constrain investors' instincts, computers can read market sentiment in real time, high-frequency transactions are conducted in milliseconds, and decentralised finance undermines conventional banking's very structure. Each of these improvements indicates a change not just in tools but also in thinking, with data driving choices, automation replacing guessing, and finance becoming as dynamic as the technology that carries it ahead.

However, as promising as these developments are, they also introduce new obstacles. This new period will be shaped by issues such as market stability, ethical concerns, and the balance between human judgement and AI's calculating capability. As AI technology improves its prediction powers and increases its reach, investors must adjust by learning how to properly use these tools without losing sight of the fundamentals. The distinction between opportunity and risk is becoming more blurred, and comprehending this changing environment will be critical to success (Boutros et al., 2020).

Finally, AI and future trends are altering finance in ways that will empower investors and transform decision-making. The possibilities are exciting, but success in this new environment will take more than access to powerful tools; it will also necessitate a thorough knowledge of how to merge technology with timeless values. As we move forward, the combination of AI and human understanding promises to produce a market that is not just quicker and smarter but also more inclusive and robust, paving the way for a new era of investment.

References

Ackert, L. F., & Deaves, R. (2009). *Behavioral finance: Psychology, decision-making, and markets*. South-Western Cengage Learning.

Baek, S., & Lee, K. Y. (2021). The risk transmission of COVID-19 in the US stock market. *Applied Economics, 53*(17), 1976–1990.

Barber, B. M., & Odean, T. (2000). Trading is hazardous to your wealth: The common stock investment performance of individual investors. *The Journal of Finance, 55*(2), 773–806.

Ben-David, I. T. Z. H. A. K., Franzoni, F., Landier, A., & Moussawi, R. (2013). Do hedge funds manipulate stock prices? *The Journal of Finance, 68*(6), 2383–2434.

Boutros, M., Ben-David, I., Graham, J. R., Harvey, C. R., & Payne, J. W. (2020). *The persistence of miscalibration*. National Bureau of Economic Research.

Glaser, M., & Weber, M. (2007). Overconfidence and trading volume: Evidence from market experiments. *Journal of Financial Markets, 10*(2), 100–130.

Hirshleifer, D. (2015). Behavioral finance. *Annual Review of Financial Economics, 7*(1), 133–159.

Kahneman, D., & Tversky, A. (1979). Prospect theory: An analysis of decision under risk. *Econometrica, 47*(2), 263–292.

Kensho. (2020). Advancements in AI-driven sentiment analysis. *Financial Innovation and AI, 23*(3), 145–160.

Königstorfer, J., & Thalmann, M. (2020). NLP-based investment insights: Enhancing returns. *Management Science Review, 45*(3), 245–270.

Liu, Y., Sun, Q., & Wu, L. (2020). Sentiment-based investment strategies: A machine learning perspective. *Journal of Behavioral Finance, 21*(4), 341–359.

Shiller, R. J. (2000). *Irrational exuberance*. Princeton University Press.

Thaler, R. H., & Sunstein, C. R. (2008). *Nudge: Improving decisions about health, wealth, and happiness*. Penguin Books.

Vasileiou, E. (2022). Behavioral finance and algorithmic trading: Understanding psychological impacts. *Behavioral Finance Review*.

Lo, A. W. (2004). Adaptive markets: A financial evolutionary theory. *Journal of Portfolio Management, 30*(5), 15–29.

Chapter 10
Behavioural Finance in a Global Context

In the vast, complex network of global finance, two separate universes emerge, each with its pulse and rhythm. Finance is a seasoned sector in industrialised nations such as the United States, United Kingdom, Japan, and Germany, where decades of expertise and cultural confidence foster steady development and cautious risk-taking. Investors here balance prudence and optimism, influenced by statistics, history, and a profound sense of stability. There's a sense of sophistication and calm confidence that propels market movements as if everyone in the room is a well-rehearsed member of a well-tuned symphony. Investors, battered by years of economic ups and downs, rely on the art of asset preservation while seeking modest returns, combining ambition with a firm commitment to tradition and stability.

On the opposite end of the scale are emerging markets, which are alive with energy, promise, and an uninhibited desire for expansion. Malaysia, Thailand, Brazil, and South Africa are at the vanguard of economic development, where the thrill of possibility is matched by a desire to embark on new endeavours. The investor mentality here is bold, unconstrained, and, at times, impulsive—a passion for immediate riches and the opportunity to rewrite financial destinies drives market psychology. These investors, who are frequently young and motivated by the revolutionary power of digital platforms, social media, and increased access to global markets, are redefining financial landscapes with each transaction. In emerging economies, behavioural finance is infused with ambition, resilience, and a desire to make up for lost time. In these opposing realms, behavioural finance shows not just how we invest but also who we are, capturing the goals, desires, and cultural fingerprints of investors throughout the world.

K. L. Ooi, *Demystifying Behavioral Finance*,
https://doi.org/10.1007/978-981-96-2690-8_10

10.1 United States: The Culture of Optimism and Risk-Taking

The financial market in the United States exudes contagious optimism and audacity. This market is characterised by high risk and significant gain, with investors eager to make large bets on ideas, technology, and persons, often disregarding financial prudence warnings. This cultural perspective has a significant impact on the behaviour of American investors, who welcome risk because they believe in the 'American Dream' and that everything is possible (Loang, 2025). Optimism fuels the overconfidence bias in US markets, where investors, seduced by success stories and encouraged by the belief that they, too, can overcome the odds, routinely overestimate their capabilities.

Overconfidence in American markets is not a subtle effect; it is the driving force behind some of the country's most spectacular financial booms. The late 1990s dot-com boom epitomised this mindset. Investors invested billions of dollars into tech businesses that had little to no income, confident that they were investing for the future. Pets.com and Webvan, despite their poor business models, were valued at billions of dollars merely because they reflected the Internet's potential. The Nasdaq skyrocketed 400% between 1995 and 2000, only to fall in a dramatic burst of overconfidence in 2000, wiping away $5 trillion in market value.

Even despite repeated economic lessons, American investors are still driven to high-risk wagers, possibly more than any other developed economy. This tendency was seen again during the subprime mortgage crisis of 2008, when confidence in everlasting development led to reckless mortgage practices and excessive lending. The American population, influenced by the myth that house ownership was a road to riches, continued to invest in housing, even when prices grew unsustainable (Glaser & Weber, 2007). When the bubble burst, the consequences were catastrophic, plunging the world economy into a recession and resulting in over $700 billion in bailouts for financial institutions. These cycles demonstrate that optimism and overconfidence are profoundly embedded in the American investment style, propelling the market to record highs and catastrophic lows.

Technology and social media have only fuelled this risk-taking behaviour. Platforms like Robinhood and platforms like Reddit's WallStreetBets foster a 'mob mentality', in which investors coalesce behind the belief that the underdog will defeat Wall Street. The GameStop debacle of 2021 highlights this: retail investors drove the stock up more than 1700% in a single month, squeezing hedge funds and producing market pandemonium. The pervasive FOMO (fear of missing out) among regular investors, mixed with a dislike for institutional investors, has resulted in a potent mix of optimism, defiance, and risk-taking. This particularly American combination is constantly reshaping the market.

10.2 The United Kingdom: Conservatism and Steadfastness in Investment Choices

British investors have a careful and disciplined attitude to the stock market, which contrasts sharply with the American mentality of reckless risk-taking. The UK financial environment is defined by a cultural inclination for stability and a long-standing respect for established organisations. British investors prioritise asset preservation above quick returns. This mindset may be traced back to the country's history of steady, gradual economic expansion, as opposed to the boom-and-bust cycles witnessed in the United States. This conservatism is firmly embedded in the British mentality, along with a significant loss aversion—the psychological preference for avoiding losses rather than earning profits (Coval & Shumway, 2005). British investors seek to avoid losses at all costs, even passing up prospective gains.

The 2008 financial crisis exposed the disparities in approach between the US and UK markets. Although both countries were impacted, British banks fared better than many of their American counterparts. This resilience may be linked to the UK's more stringent regulatory system and cautious banking culture. British banks were more careful with their lending standards and did not embrace subprime lending to the same level. UK investors, for their part, shunned some of the more risky ventures, owing to the British propensity for prudence and pragmatism when dealing with risk. In reality, UK banks needed significantly less bailout money, with the British government paying roughly £137 billion vs. the $700 billion bailout in the United States, indicating a more conservative financial culture.

Another distinguishing characteristic of British investor behaviour is a preference for blue-chip firms and dividend income. The United Kingdom has a long history of income-focused investment, with many British pension funds investing heavily in firms that pay out regular dividends. British investors tend to consider investments as sources of income rather than speculative potential for huge profits (Baker & Ricciardi, 2014). This approach reflects a more significant societal preference for financial restraint. Dividend-paying companies in industries such as utilities, telecoms, and pharmaceuticals dominate UK portfolios, enabling British investors to generate consistent income while avoiding speculative, high-risk investments.

However, this careful approach has several limitations. British investors often lose out on development possibilities, especially in high-growth technology areas that they see as erratic and hazardous. In 2021, tech stocks contributed considerably to global market gains, with the US tech sector increasing by more than 30%, while the UK's FTSE 100, which is dominated by conventional sectors, increased at a slower rate of roughly 14%. This contrast highlights the cost of a cautious attitude since British investors may forego development in favour of security. Nonetheless, the British propensity for safety and stability continues to affect the market, fostering a financial culture in which modest, consistent returns are seen as the hallmark of intelligent investment.

10.3 Japan: A Legacy of Caution and Resilience Amid Economic Stagnation

Japanese investors work in a financial environment characterised by a deep sense of prudence, a result of the country's economic history and cultural norms. Japanese culture values stability, collectivism, and humility, all of which have a substantial impact on investing behaviour. Japanese investors are often risk-averse, prioritising capital protection above large profits. This conservative worldview was strengthened by Japan's 'Lost Decade' in the 1990s, a period of protracted economic stagnation that saw the stock market crash and the real estate market slump. Even now, Japan's primary stock index, the Nikkei 225, has partially recovered from its high of more than 30 years ago.

This economic background has made Japanese investors very apprehensive of high-risk projects (An et al., 2020). While American and European investors are increasingly interested in high-tech equities and digital assets, Japanese portfolios remain focused on conventional sectors like manufacturing, medicines, and real estate. Bonds, especially government-issued bonds, are a vital component of Japanese investment portfolios, showing a high loss aversion attitude. In reality, cash and bank deposits account for more than half of all household assets in Japan, compared to 14% in the United States. This desire for liquidity and safety over development exemplifies Japan's conservative financial culture, in which the fear of loss surpasses the appeal of prospective benefits.

Japanese investors are also significantly impacted by regret aversion, which is the inclination to avoid taking actions that may cause regret. This leads to a risk-averse investing attitude, with many Japanese people preferring 'buy-and-hold' methods that represent a long-term, steady mentality. For example, during the 2008 global financial crisis, Japanese investors were more cautious than their Western counterparts, lowering their exposure to stocks and withdrawing to safer assets such as bonds. The attitude was less about capitalising on a down market and more about safeguarding existing wealth—a distinguishing aspect of Japan's conservative investing strategy.

Japan's collectivist society reinforces this risk-averse mindset. Japanese investors often engage in herd behaviour; however, unlike speculative bubbles observed in the United States or developing markets, this herd behaviour pushes investors to safer assets during times of market stress. When the COVID-19 epidemic started in early 2020, Japanese investors shifted to government bonds and cash savings, preferring safety over speculative returns. This careful change is indicative of a deeply ingrained cultural preference for group agreement and security. Even when global markets recovered, Japanese investors took longer to return to stocks, reflecting Japan's financial conservatism in terms of risk and reward.

10.4 Germany: The Market of Order, Rationality, and Endurance

The German financial market is characterised by discipline, logic, and a dedication to stability that permeates all aspects of investing. German investors are among the most conservative in Europe, preferring solid, low-risk investments over speculative opportunities. A historical sensitivity to volatility has shaped Germany's financial culture, dating back to the 1920s hyperinflation and the economic destruction of WWII. These events left an indelible effect on German financial psychology, instilling a feeling of caution that continues strong to this day.

German investors have a solid domestic bias, investing primarily in firms they know and trust. This preference for known assets is due in part to a strong trust and familiarity bias, with German corporations such as Siemens, BASF, and Allianz seen as secure, dependable investments. In reality, German investors devote a significant chunk of their portfolios to local shares, notably in the industrial, automotive, and engineering industries. According to a 2021 survey, more than 60% of German retail investors owned significant investments in German blue-chip companies, which is in sharp contrast to the diversified, multinational portfolios often seen in US and UK markets.

The German market is also distinctive in its emphasis on socially responsible investment. Ethical investing techniques are becoming more popular among German investors, who choose sustainable and ecologically sensitive enterprises. This emphasis reflects a larger cultural ideal of social responsibility and a commitment to ethical financial practices. German investors are more likely to invest in ESG (environmental, social, and governance)—compliant funds than their counterparts in other nations, with Germany accounting for more than 30% of Europe's ESG fund assets by 2022. This commitment to sustainable finance reflects the values-driven attitude of German investors, who see financial returns as just one component of the investing equation.

While this conservative, socially concerned strategy has advantages, it may prevent German investors from capitalising on high-growth possibilities. The meteoric surge of tech stocks and cryptocurrencies has sparked scepticism in Germany, where investors value safety above speculation. The German stock market increased by around 12% in 2021, whereas the Nasdaq, which is mainly geared towards technology, increased by more than 26%. This difference demonstrates the disadvantage of a conservative approach: although Germany's concentration on stability protects its investors against volatility, it may restrict prospective rewards during bull markets.

10.5 Canada: Balancing Caution with Opportunity in the Great White North

Canadian investors find a unique balance between prudence and opportunity, reflecting a mix of British conservatism and American optimism. With strong cultural and economic links to both countries, Canada's financial sector incorporates features of each, producing an atmosphere in which investors are both pragmatic and receptive to new ideas. The Canadian market is strongly dominated by income-producing assets, notably dividend-paying equities in industries such as banking, natural resources, and real estate. This emphasis on income stability above capital gains is a distinguishing trait of Canadian investing behaviour.

The Canadian regulatory framework has a considerable impact on investor behaviour. Canada is well known for its stable banking industry, which includes some of the world's safest financial institutions, fostering confidence and encouraging conservative investment. During the 2008 financial crisis, Canadian banks fared reasonably well, thanks to cautious lending procedures, which protected Canadian investors from the brunt of the consequences. This resiliency has bolstered Canadian investors' trust in their local financial system, resulting in a substantial home bias in which Canadian shares, particularly in the banking and oil industries, comprise a significant portion of investment portfolios.

However, Canadian investors are open to innovation. The closeness to the US technological industry has impacted Canadian perceptions towards technology and development potential. As digital platforms gain popularity, Canadian investors are exhibiting an increasing interest in sectors such as technology and healthcare. As they seek to mix cautious investments with exposure to high-growth areas, a rising number of Canadians are turning to exchange-traded funds (ETFs) and robo-advisors. As of 2022, Canada has over $300 billion in ETF assets. This development illustrates Canada's growing financial culture, which welcomes new possibilities while maintaining financial security.

The Canadian market also has a distinct emphasis on socially responsible investing, with Canadian investors increasingly gravitating to ESG-focused products. Canada's dedication to environmental preservation is reflected in its financial industry, where sustainable investments are seen as ethically and financially advantageous. This move towards sustainable finance has gained traction in recent years, with Canadian ESG assets exceeding $30 billion by 2021, demonstrating the rising importance of ethical investment in Canadian portfolios. This combined emphasis on security and sustainability embodies the core of Canadian investor behaviour, which combines prudence with a readiness to explore new areas.

10.6 Malaysia: Tradition Meets a New Wave of Young Investors

Malaysia's financial environment is deeply rooted in tradition, with investing decisions influenced by a desire for stability, family values, and, for many, adherence to Islamic finance principles. For years, Malaysian investors have depended mainly on physical assets such as real estate and cash holdings, reflecting a cultural conservatism and a desire for safe, long-term investments. However, Malaysia is one of Southeast Asia's most active financial markets. In recent years, there has been an influx of younger, tech-savvy investors who are questioning old standards and redefining the market.

One of the significant effects on Malaysian investor behaviour is the widespread adoption of Islamic financing, which encourages ethical investing practices while discouraging speculative or overly leveraged activity. Malaysia is a worldwide pioneer in Islamic finance, with a significant component of its stock market classified as Shariah-compliant. Approximately 64% of Bursa Malaysia-listed businesses follow Shariah rules, giving investors a variety of alternatives that line with their ethical and religious convictions. This has instilled a cautious orientation to risk since speculative trading is usually banned under Islamic finance norms. Shariah-compliant investment prioritises businesses such as healthcare, technology, and manufacturing while guiding investors away from more volatile and ethically questionable sectors like gambling and alcohol.

The younger generation, on the other hand, is more eager to experiment with risky assets, particularly now that digital trading platforms have made the stock market more accessible. The advent of platforms such as Rakuten Trade and MIDF Invest has increased retail investors, with more than 40% of these newcomers under the age of 30. These youthful investors, influenced by social media and the worldwide move to digital finance, are more willing to dabble with a variety of assets, including ETFs, overseas shares, and even cryptocurrencies. This transition has revolutionised Malaysia's typically conservative market, instilling vitality that contrasts with previous generations' cautious investment decisions.

Herd behaviour has been more evident among Malaysian retail investors, particularly when they rush to industries seen as high growth. During the COVID-19 pandemic, for example, glove manufacturing stocks saw exceptional interest as worldwide demand for personal protective equipment (PPE) increased. Companies such as Top Glove and Hartalega saw price increases fuelled by retail investors after social media buzz, only to see significant drops as demand levelled out. This behaviour highlights a rising FOMO (fear of missing out) mindset among young Malaysian investors, who are eager to embrace short-term opportunities while frequently underestimating the dangers involved.

Malaysian investors, regardless of age, still choose physical assets, with real estate being a popular investment option. Real estate is seen as a trustworthy store of value, and Malaysian households commonly invest in it as a means of wealth preservation. However, government cooling measures, increasing real estate prices, and a shifting economic environment have prompted some younger investors to seek profits in other sectors, including digital assets and technology companies. This trend reflects a rising desire for development prospects, but a cultural focus on family-oriented financial planning and prudent asset accumulation balances it.

10.7 Singapore: High Financial Literacy and a Globalised Investment Approach

Singaporeans approach investment with pragmatism and strong financial literacy, making them among Asia's most intelligent investors. Singapore's prominence as an economic centre, along with its well-regulated markets, has created an atmosphere in which investors may confidently navigate both local and foreign markets. Many Singaporeans prioritise wealth growth, and they handle their money with a systematic, long-term view (Loang, 2025). The city-state's distinct regulatory structure, in which both the public and commercial sectors promote financial education, has resulted in a populace that approaches investing choices with a measured, disciplined perspective.

Singapore's obligatory savings and retirement system, the Central Provident Fund (CPF), has a significant impact on investing behaviour. CPF payments from both workers and employers provide a considerable safety net, encouraging disciplined saving and a long-term emphasis on financial stability. Singaporeans may invest their CPF savings in authorised funds, shares, and bonds under the CPF Investment Scheme, providing an extra incentive for prudent, diversified investing. This approach has a significant impact on investor behaviour because it promotes a mentality that values wealth preservation and slow expansion above speculative profits.

Despite this conservative base, Singaporean investors, especially the younger generation, have embraced technology and high-growth investments. Digital trading services like Tiger Brokers and robo-advisors like StashAway have grown in popularity, allowing ordinary investors to access both local and international markets with low costs. This tech-savvy populace is growing interested in areas like technology, biotech, and sustainable finance, indicating a trend towards contemporary, innovative enterprises. For example, during the worldwide cryptocurrency bubble in 2021, Singapore observed a massive increase in crypto investments among young investors, fuelled by the promise of quick returns and FOMO.

Singapore's high housing prices also influence investment decisions. Real estate is seen as a very desired asset, not just for its long-term appreciation potential but also as a sign of stability and social standing. Despite government cooling measures aimed at reducing speculative purchasing, property remains a crucial component of Singaporean wealth-building schemes. Private residential property prices in Singapore increased by more than 10% in 2021, demonstrating a widespread belief in real estate's long-term worth. For many Singaporeans, investing in property is both a financial and cultural choice, and it is seen as a haven even during times of market instability.

Singaporeans have excellent financial knowledge, but they are not immune to herd behaviour, particularly in high-demand sectors like real estate and, more recently, technology equities. Online investing groups and social media platforms have exacerbated the impact of herd mentality, resulting in speculative spikes in specific industries. Singaporeans' readiness to invest in both domestic and global markets demonstrates an intelligent strategy, mixing prudent decisions with selective risk-taking in high-growth sectors.

10.8 Thailand: Youthful Enthusiasm and Community Dynamics

Thailand's financial scene is one of fast change and great energy, propelled by a youthful, ambitious populace eager to participate in the stock market and alternative assets. Thai investors, especially the younger generation, are more receptive to speculative trading than their counterparts in neighbouring nations. This is attributable in part to the country's dynamic economic climate, in which growing urbanisation and digital change provide new profit possibilities on a regular basis. However, this risk-taking mentality often results in increased market volatility, as Thai investors seek short-term profits without fully accounting for prospective losses.

The Thai market's accessibility, along with the rising popularity of digital trading platforms, has helped to attract a new generation of retail investors. During the COVID-19 epidemic, platforms like Streaming and Settrade experienced an increase in activity as young investors joined the market in droves. In 2020, retail investors accounted for more than 50% of trading volume on Thailand's Stock Exchange, a considerable rise from prior years. This flood of new investors has resulted in a significant amount of speculative trading as young Thais attempt to profit from market changes. The Thai stock market is often characterised by large trading volumes and a short-term emphasis, with famous firms seeing considerable price changes as ordinary investors enter and exit holdings.

Social media has a significant impact on Thai investor behaviour, instilling a feeling of community and collective action that reinforces herd mentality. Investing clubs and online communities on platforms such as Facebook and Line have a significant impact on investing choices since participants routinely exchange advice, debate market trends, and promote group purchasing. This communal approach often results in synchronised market behaviour, with certain companies or sectors seeing quick price gains based on community agreement rather than essential study. For example, when worldwide demand for electric cars increased, Thai investors rushed to associated equities, sending prices dramatically higher.

Thai investors are enthusiastic about speculative assets, including cryptocurrencies, which have established a significant presence in the nation. In 2021, Thailand reported a record 600,000 Bitcoin trading accounts, double the amount from the previous year. Despite warnings from Thailand's Securities and Exchange Commission, digital assets continue to entice youthful investors. For many, Bitcoin provides a chance to make fast money in a market that seems more accessible and more profitable than conventional assets. However, this speculative enthusiasm exposes Thai investors to high market volatility since many buy digital assets without fully comprehending the dangers.

Despite their willingness to speculate, Thai investors have a cultural appreciation for physical goods, with gold being a prevalent investment. Gold is considered a culturally important item in Thailand, representing prosperity and security. During economic downturns or periods of political instability, Thai investors typically resort to gold as a haven, giving stability in a chaotic market. The dependence on gold reflects a more significant cultural emphasis on wealth preservation, contrasting the high-risk behaviour observed in equities and digital assets with a strong preference for long-term value.

As we stand back and examine these financial landscapes, we discover an intriguing truth: although established and emerging economies seem to be worlds apart, they are linked by the same human instincts that drive us all. Investors are bound by common biases in both the structured, data-driven markets of the West and the busy, fast-expanding exchanges of Southeast Asia and beyond—a desire for achievement, a fear of loss, and the search for security. Behavioural finance has revealed that whether we're in New York, Bangkok, Tokyo, or Kuala Lumpur, we're all impacted by the same emotions and tales about opportunity and danger. The patterns and scales may change, but at our core, we are all motivated by the same impulses, battling with similar fears and desires, reacting to the demands of a market that both challenges and rewards.

However, it is in the contrasts that the brilliance of behavioural finance is fully shown. Developed markets, with their seasoned intelligence, demonstrate the need for restraint, prudence, and measured risk. They are distinguished by their resilience, long-term perspective, and devotion to stability. In contrast, emerging markets are alive with the raw energy of opportunity, where the desire for rapid victories and transformational benefits paints the financial landscape in bright, unexpected colours. These markets form a worldwide mosaic—a tapestry that illustrates the dynamic, ever-changing essence of finance. As we look forward, these two worlds will continue to learn from one another, combining the wisdom of the past with the bold energy of the new. And in this dance of opposites, the future of behavioural finance will be written—a future that honours both stability and ambition, prudence and boldness, demonstrating that no matter where we invest, the narrative of money is ultimately a human tale.

References

Ackert, L. F., & Deaves, R. (2009). *Behavioral finance: Psychology, decision-making, and markets*. South-Western Cengage Learning.

An, L., Wang, H., Wang, J., & Yu, J. (2020). Lottery-related anomalies: The role of reference-dependent preferences. *Management Science, 66*(1), 473–501.

Baker, H. K., & Ricciardi, V. (2014). Behavioral aspects of financial planning and investing. *Management Research Review, 37*(10), 818–828.

Barber, B. M., & Odean, T. (2000). Trading is hazardous to your wealth: The common stock investment performance of individual investors. *The Journal of Finance, 55*(2), 773–806.

Barberis, N., Shleifer, A., & Vishny, R. (1998). A model of investor sentiment. *Journal of Financial Economics, 49*(3), 307–343.

Benartzi, S., & Thaler, R. H. (1995). Myopic loss aversion and the equity premium puzzle. *The Quarterly Journal of Economics, 110*(1), 73–92.

Bikhchandani, S., Hirshleifer, D., & Welch, I. (1992). A theory of fads, fashion, custom, and cultural change as informational cascades. *Journal of Political Economy, 100*(5), 992–1026.

Camerer, C. F., & Loewenstein, G. (2004). Behavioral economics: Past, present, future. In *Advances in behavioral economics* (pp. 3–51). Princeton University Press.

Coval, J. D., & Shumway, T. (2005). Do behavioral biases affect prices? *The Journal of Finance, 60*(1), 1–34.

Daniel, K., Hirshleifer, D., & Subrahmanyam, A. (1998). Investor psychology and security market under-and overreactions. *The Journal of Finance, 53*(6), 1839–1885.

Glaser, M., & Weber, M. (2007). Overconfidence and trading volume: Evidence from market experiments. *Journal of Financial Markets, 10*(2), 100–130.

Loang, O. K. (2025). Can herding be adaptive? Evidence from markets sentiment, news sentiment and happiness in global energy markets. Millennial Asia, 09763996241313001.

Shiller, R. J. (2000). *Irrational exuberance*. Princeton University Press.

Thaler, R. H., & Sunstein, C. R. (2008). *Nudge: Improving decisions about health, wealth, and happiness*. Penguin Books.

Wurgler, J., & Baker, M. (2006). Investor sentiment and the cross-section of stock returns. *The Journal of Finance, 61*(4), 1645–1680.

Chapter 11
Policy Implications and Future Directions

We are on the verge of a financial revolution, one that will rewrite the rules and reshape how we interact with money, risk, and opportunities. Gone are the days when markets belonged to a select few on Wall Street; now, finance is in the hands of everyone with a smartphone, a trading app, or an interest in cryptocurrency. But with this tremendous power comes a world of complexity, where the perils are as many as the opportunities. Artificial intelligence analyses every transaction, computers execute orders in milliseconds, and social media may transform a stock into a phenomenon overnight. As the frontiers of finance grow, the task is not just to keep up but also to build a financial ecosystem that is strong, fair, and imaginative.

In this last chapter, we examine the future of finance in three key areas: employing AI to safeguard and assist investors, integrating worldwide rules to create a smooth, accessible market, and applying behavioural insights to make retirement planning a natural, joyful part of life. These are more than simply concepts; they represent the cornerstone of a financial universe in which innovation and integrity coexist, technology complements knowledge, and the investor's experience is governed as much by empathy as by algorithms. This is the future we're creating: one in which money is more than simply a transaction but also a vehicle for empowerment, security, and social progress.

11.1 Enhanced Disclosure Requirements for Retail Investment Platforms

Imagine entering a virtual trading platform for the first time. It's elegant and user-friendly and allows you to trade with the flick of a finger. However, for many inexperienced investors, that swipe may hold hazards beyond their comprehension (Malmendier & Nagel, 2011). Today's retail platforms must evolve from

K. L. Ooi, *Demystifying Behavioral Finance*,
https://doi.org/10.1007/978-981-96-2690-8_11

transactional conduits to pillars of education and protection, beginning with more vital disclosure rules that make investors fully aware of what is at risk.

Present disclosure methods are often hidden in the dense text, laden with jargon that most users scan if they read at all. Consider a platform where disclosures come to life, complete with interactive elements that gently remind consumers of the dangers before they finalise a deal. When someone is about to undertake a high-risk transaction, a visual alert may emerge, displaying, for example, a timeline of usual outcomes for comparable deals. It may even contain a short 'cool-off' period to encourage consumers to stop before making risky bets. According to research, even a few seconds of thought may minimise impulsive transactions by up to 20%, giving investors time to ponder before committing.

By including behavioural 'nudges', these platforms might promote an educated decision-making culture. Consider a system that adjusts screen colours or provides personalised risk estimates based on prior transactions. The purpose is not to discourage investment but rather to guarantee that consumers fully grasp the possible ramifications of their decisions. Policies mandating such disclosures have the potential to substantially redefine the retail platform experience, transforming it from high-speed trading arenas to places of contemplation in which users are urged to think critically about each decision. In a world where FOMO and rapid satisfaction drive behaviour, these increased disclosures would serve as a subtle reminder to think long term.

11.2 Regulating Social Media's Influence on Trading Behaviour

Social media has become the new town square of finance, where market trends emerge, morph, and propagate at breakneck speed. It's a place where a popular tweet or Reddit post may spark frenetic trading, propelling equities to stunning highs or lows within hours. For every success story, there is a cautionary tale, as naive investors get drawn into trends they don't comprehend. The need for legislation here is not to stifle free expression but to provide transparency and accountability to a sector with immense power over financial markets.

Imagine if social media influencers, particularly those with large followings, were compelled to reveal any financial relationships or stakes in the businesses they advocate. A discreet transparency warning, similar to those seen in health-related material, may appear alongside financial pieces, informing viewers that their views may be financially driven. Consider the GameStop saga: what if viewers knew upfront if their favourite influencers stood to benefit from the stock's rise? It may have provided perspective, preventing hundreds of impetuous transactions based only on viral buzz (Hirshleifer & Shumway, 2003).

Furthermore, platforms may add financial 'risk alerts' similar to the labelling seen on high-caffeine energy drinks or specific medical cautions. For example, postings on volatile stocks, options, or cryptocurrency may include a risk advisory advising visitors to proceed with care. These warnings would not interfere with the content but would serve as a reminder that financial choices need careful consideration. According to a recent CFA Institute research, 60% of retail investors have traded in response to social media trends, highlighting the potential effect of even basic notifications. With regulations that promote openness and informed decision-making, we can create a digital ecosystem in which investors interact with finance mindfully even while traversing the fast-paced world of social media.

11.3 Restrictions on High-Frequency and Algorithmic Trading

High-frequency trading (HFT) and algorithmic trading have transformed the financial industry into a hyperefficient and competitive battlefield. The advantages are undeniable: more liquidity, reduced spreads, and quicker execution. However, the drawbacks are visible, particularly during unpredictable times. The notorious 2010 'Flash Crash' is a sobering example, in which the Dow Jones fell over 1000 points in minutes, spurred by a perfect storm of automated trading and panic-driven sell-offs. Individual investors may be devastated by such swings and the algorithms that cause them to work with a ruthless disregard for human interests.

To reduce HFT's disruptive potential, officials should implement 'speed bumps' during moments of extreme volatility. These automatic delays, even if just for a fraction of a second, would prohibit trading algorithms from executing in large numbers, allowing markets time to stabilise. Consider it as providing friction to a runaway train, a system that slows things down when velocity gets unsafe. Similarly, mandating HFT businesses to publish specific trading patterns or risk management measures might increase openness, enabling regulators and the public to understand better how these algorithms perform under pressure (Hirshleifer, 2015).

Beyond speed limitations, implementing 'circuit breakers' that block trading for certain assets during flash crashes might help safeguard the market from severe volatility. Consider a system that temporarily suspends trading in a stock if the price moves by more than a particular percentage in seconds. Such regulations serve as shock absorbers, safeguarding both ordinary investors and the market's integrity. By enforcing these constraints, authorities would create a more humane market, one in which technology is used as an aid rather than a danger, and stability takes priority over constant speed.

11.4 Promoting ESG and Ethical Investment Standards

As the financial sector becomes more accountable, environmental, social, and governance investment has evolved from a niche interest to a worldwide imperative. Over $35 trillion in assets is now committed to ESG investments globally, demonstrating a rising awareness of firms' effect on society and the environment. However, as ESG gets more prominent, the possibility of 'greenwashing'—companies claiming to be sustainable but not taking actual action—increases. To encourage authentic ESG practices, policymakers must intervene to guarantee that investors can trust the principles behind their investments.

Policymakers might start by adopting standardised, mandated ESG measurements that require corporations to publicly report their environmental, social, and governance activities in a measured and verifiable manner. Consider a framework that allows investors to assess firms based not just on revenue or profit but also on their carbon impact, diversity efforts, and ethical labour practices. By establishing a standard, ESG investment might evolve from a marketing gimmick to an accurate indicator of a company's commitment to sound change. For example, corporations that meet or surpass these requirements may be eligible for tax breaks, encouraging them to adopt policies that benefit both shareholders and society.

To emphasise the relevance of ESG, governments may include these principles in national retirement funds, enabling individuals to grow their retirement savings via investments that reflect their beliefs. Public pension funds might prioritise ESG-compliant enterprises, boosting sustainable development and demonstrating a national commitment to ethical finance. Independently verified ESG ratings might assist retail investors in making more informed choices, ensuring that 'sustainable' investments have a meaningful social and environmental effect (Glaser & Weber, 2007). By incorporating ESG into the fabric of financial policy, we pave the way for a new age in which profits and purpose coexist, transforming finance into a force for good in a society that sorely needs it.

11.5 AI-Based Investor Protection Tools

Imagine a future in which your financial app is more than simply a trading tool; it is a personal assistant that alerts you to trends in your behaviour that may lead to unsafe choices. This is the promise of AI-based investor protection tools—a paradigm shift in how we interact with finance in which artificial intelligence not only drives market forecasts but actively protects investors. In the future, your trading platform may detect when you are sliding into behavioural traps, such as overtrading or pursuing short-term profits, and recommend more balanced tactics based on your financial objectives and risk tolerance.

For example, an AI-powered tool may recognise when an investor is in a trading frenzy, fuelled by the highs of a recent victory or the lows of a recent loss. Instead of just enabling the next transaction, the tool may provide a mild prompt: 'Would you like to review your portfolio performance this month?' By tapping into these behavioural clues, AI may function as a 'behavioural coach', assisting investors in making more thoughtful rather than impulsive choices. A 2022 research found that users of platforms with built-in AI assistance decreased impulsive transactions by up to 30%, highlighting AI's potential to change the way we invest.

Looking forward, AI-powered investor protection systems may grow to include deep learning models that analyse market situations and adapt suggestions appropriately. Consider an app that informs you when market volatility is high and recommends alternate tactics that correspond with long-term objectives rather than following erratic patterns (Baker & Ricciardi, 2014). By incorporating these technologies, future trading platforms may go beyond transaction-based models, becoming full-fledged financial companions that enable investors to flourish rather than merely trade.

11.6 Global Harmonisation of Financial Regulations

In a world where markets cross borders, financial regulation needs to be more cohesive, with individual nations implementing their regulations frequently in ways that do not reflect the reality of global trade. Consider a Japanese investor trading equities on a US platform while managing various tax, regulatory, and legal limitations. For the contemporary investor, such a landscape is complicated, expensive, and, at times, overwhelming. Global harmonisation of financial rules would result in a more uniform and streamlined framework, making cross-border investment easier and safer.

A worldwide 'financial code of conduct' might set criteria for transparency, ethical investing, and responsible trading. This does not imply enforcing the same standards everywhere but rather establishing a framework on which nations may develop their own distinctive, culturally appropriate legislation. For example, although ESG (environmental, social, and governance) standards may become global, governments may be able to tailor particular indicators to suit local values and environmental goals.

The European Union's General Data Protection Regulation (GDPR) serves as an example, illustrating how cross-border legal frameworks may protect individual rights while promoting uniformity. Imagine a comparable approach to financial regulation in which nations agree on fundamental concepts such as investor protection, anti-money laundering, and market openness. The advantages would be significant: lower compliance costs for worldwide businesses, more straightforward tax reporting for individual investors, and a more accessible international market. According to a recent Globe Bank analysis, a harmonised regulatory framework could increase global investment flows by 15%, offering a considerable economic boost while making financing more accessible to investors throughout the globe.

11.7 Behavioural Nudges in Retirement Planning

For many people, retirement planning is an abstract goal that seems far away and easy to put off. Behavioural finance research has revealed that individuals often underestimate their future requirements in favour of immediate incentives and short-term profits. But what if retirement planning could use behavioural nudges to make saving seem natural, easy, and even enjoyable? Consider a retirement plan that adjusts to your life's milestones, such as encouraging you to contribute more when you earn a raise or recommending a diverse portfolio as you near retirement age.

One of the most successful behavioural finance initiatives has been 'auto-enrollment', which involves automatically enrolling workers in retirement savings programmes unless they opt out. According to research conducted by the National Bureau of Economic Research, auto-enrollment improves participation rates by up to 80%. However, the future of retirement planning may extend these insights much further. For example, 'auto-escalation' might gradually boost payments over time, adapting to income growth and life events. An app might push users with messages such as, 'Your salary increased by 5% this year—would you like to save a little more for your future?'

These behavioural nudges may also help to improve portfolio balance. A recent trend is the adoption of AI-powered retirement solutions that monitor market fluctuations and provide timely recommendations. For example, if an investor's portfolio becomes unduly focused on a particular industry, a gentle reminder may recommend reallocating assets to maintain a diversified approach. Such nudges fit with long-term aims and prevent retirees from making rash decisions during market downturns. Policymakers may encourage firms to use these tools by providing tax breaks for businesses that include behavioural nudges into their retirement plans, ensuring that more individuals retire with the resources they need.

As we close the book on today's financial reality, the future is wide open, with the possibility to construct markets that are smarter, kinder, and more resilient. These next steps—using AI to safeguard investors, developing a uniform global regulatory framework, and integrating retirement planning into daily life—are more than just policy reforms. They are an invitation to rethink money as something more significant: a force that empowers, protects, and develops with us, no matter what our ambitions or where we are.

This is the centre of tomorrow's financial landscape—a location where technology broadens our knowledge, investors travel confidently across markets, and finance is about both opportunity and responsibility. As we enter this new period, we are creating a future in which finance leads rather than reacts, where every investor shares a common vision and where the quest for profit does not trump the pursuit of purpose. The trip ahead is both ambitious and doable, and it promises progress for every one of us—not only in numbers but also in purpose and worth. In the future of finance, the opportunities are limitless, and we are all welcome to prosper.

Behavioural finance has redefined how financial markets and decision-making processes are understood, presenting a nuanced perspective that integrates human psychology with economics. It challenges the traditional view of finance as a domain governed solely by rationality and efficiency, offering instead a vision where emotions, biases, and cognitive tendencies play central roles. This transformative approach does not merely critique traditional models; it enriches them, uncovering the human elements that drive financial behaviour and market dynamics.

At its core, behavioural finance highlights the inherent imperfections in human decision-making. Traditional financial theories often assume that market participants act logically, process information accurately, and make decisions to optimise outcomes. However, real-world evidence consistently reveals otherwise. Behavioural finance explores how cognitive biases such as overconfidence, herd behaviour, and loss aversion influence individuals and, collectively, create patterns that ripple through financial markets. These biases contribute to phenomena such as asset bubbles, abrupt market corrections, and heightened volatility, reshaping the narrative of market behaviour from one of pure logic to one influenced deeply by human nature.

Applications of behavioural finance have had widespread and tangible effects. Its principles have revolutionised the design of financial products, policies, and investment strategies. Concepts such as 'nudges' have transformed retirement savings systems, helping individuals save more effectively through mechanisms like automatic enrollment and incremental contribution increases. These strategies leverage natural tendencies such as inertia and the aversion to perceived losses, guiding individuals toward better financial decisions. Financial institutions and policymakers have embraced these insights, creating frameworks that align financial behaviours with long-term well-being.

Investment strategies also benefit from behavioural finance, with tools developed to account for emotional responses to risk and reward. Behavioural portfolio construction reflects the reality that investors are influenced by psychological factors as much as financial metrics. Risk management, informed by an understanding of fear and greed, has become more dynamic, allowing institutions to anticipate market responses during times of crisis. The influence of behavioural finance on investment practices showcases its practical value in bridging the gap between theory and application.

More than just influencing individual practices, behavioural finance has reshaped how financial markets themselves are perceived. Markets are no longer seen as purely mechanistic systems but as complex ecosystems shaped by the collective psychology of participants. This perspective helps explain why financial anomalies persist, why market cycles often include dramatic booms and busts, and why crises can escalate rapidly when panic sets in. The recognition of these patterns has created a richer understanding of market behaviour, emphasising that financial systems are as much a reflection of human behaviour as they are of economic conditions.

Looking ahead, behavioural finance will continue shaping the future of finance, especially as technology introduces new dynamics into decision-making. The rise of artificial intelligence, machine learning, and big data has transformed how information is processed, but these tools are not immune to the influence of human biases. Algorithms inherit the tendencies of their creators, reflecting the behavioural patterns embedded in their design and the data they analyse. The principles of behavioural finance provide a framework to recognise and mitigate these issues, ensuring that technological advancements align with sound decision-making.

Behavioural finance also holds immense potential for addressing broader societal challenges. Issues such as financial inequality, low savings rates, and inadequate investment habits require solutions informed by an understanding of human behaviour. Financial education initiatives rooted in behavioural principles can foster better habits, while policies designed to overcome psychological barriers to sustainable investing can promote alignment between individual actions and global goals. These efforts highlight the power of behavioural finance to create systemic change.

The legacy of behavioural finance lies in its ability to harmonise the analytical with the human. It recognises the complexities of decision-making, working within the realities of emotional and cognitive influences rather than attempting to eliminate them. This pragmatic approach has enriched academic discussions and empowered individuals and organisations to navigate the financial landscape more effectively.

As this exploration of behavioural finance concludes, its far-reaching significance becomes evident. It provides a lens for interpreting the unpredictable, understanding the interplay between logic and emotion, and navigating uncertainty with greater insight. At its heart, behavioural finance emphasises that markets and financial systems are human constructs, shaped as much by psychology as economics. The principles it offers are not just tools for better financial outcomes but a deeper understanding of the human experience within economic systems.

Behavioural finance is not just a framework for explaining irrationality; it is a guide for managing it. It reflects the stories of ambition, fear, resilience, and vulnerability that underlie every financial decision and market movement. This perspective ensures that behavioural finance will remain relevant, evolving alongside technology and markets, and continuing to inspire new approaches to understanding and managing the complexities of finance. Its ultimate impact lies in its humanity, offering a richer, more empathetic understanding of a world often reduced to numbers and equations.

References

Ackert, L. F., & Deaves, R. (2009). *Behavioral finance: Psychology, decision-making, and markets*. South-Western Cengage Learning.

Baker, H. K., & Ricciardi, V. (2014). Behavioral aspects of financial planning and investing. *Management Research Review, 37*(10), 818–828.

Barber, B. M., & Odean, T. (2000). Trading is hazardous to your wealth: The common stock investment performance of individual investors. *The Journal of Finance, 55*(2), 773–806.

Benartzi, S., & Thaler, R. H. (1995). Myopic loss aversion and the equity premium puzzle. *The Quarterly Journal of Economics, 110*(1), 73–92.

Boutros, M., Ben-David, I., Graham, J. R., Harvey, C. R., & Payne, J. W. (2020). *The persistence of miscalibration*. National Bureau of Economic Research.

Glaser, M., & Weber, M. (2007). Overconfidence and trading volume: Evidence from market experiments. *Journal of Financial Markets, 10*(2), 100–130.

Hirshleifer, D. (2015). Behavioral finance. *Annual Review of Financial Economics, 7*(1), 133–159.

Hirshleifer, D., & Shumway, T. (2003). Good day sunshine: Stock returns and the weather. *The Journal of Finance, 58*(3), 1009–1032.

Kahneman, D., & Tversky, A. (1979). Prospect theory: An analysis of decision under risk. *Econometrica, 47*(2), 263–292.

Kensho. (2020). Advancements in AI-driven sentiment analysis. *Financial Innovation and AI, 23*(3), 145–160.

Liu, Y., Sun, Q., & Wu, L. (2020). Sentiment-based investment strategies: A machine learning perspective. *Journal of Behavioral Finance, 21*(4), 341–359.

Malmendier, U., & Nagel, S. (2011). Depression babies: Do macroeconomic experiences affect risk-taking? *The Quarterly Journal of Economics, 126*(1), 373–416.

Shiller, R. J. (2000). *Irrational exuberance*. Princeton University Press.

Thaler, R. H., & Sunstein, C. R. (2008). *Nudge: Improving decisions about health, wealth, and happiness*. Penguin Books.

Wurgler, J., & Baker, M. (2006). Investor sentiment and the cross-section of stock returns. *The Journal of Finance, 61*(4), 1645–1680.

